WHY SHOULD I BE A PRODUCT MANAGER?

SHUAIB AKIYODE

Copyright © 2024. All Rights Reserved.

WHY I SHOULD BE A PRODUCT MANAGER?

No part of this publication may be reproduced, distributed, or transmitted in any form or by any means, including photocopying, recording, or any other electronic or mechanical methods, without prior written permission from the copyright owner.

This material is provided for educational and informational purposes only. It is not intended to serve as financial advice.

The author and publisher do not endorse any commercial products or services linked to this book.

Globally Available

ISBN: 978-8-3038-7915-8

A catalogue record for this book is available at the National Library of Nigeria.

TABLE OF CONTENTS

PREFACE .... **IV**

DEDICATION .... **VI**

CHAPTER ONE: WELCOME TO PRODUCT MANAGEMENT 1

CHAPTER TWO: UNDERSTANDING THE PRODCUT LIFECYCLE 10

CHAPTER THREE: SKILLS AND QUALITIES OF A PRODUCT MANAGER 19

CHAPTER FOUR: BUILDING AND LEADING CROSS-FUCTIONAL TEAMS 29

CHAPTER FIVE: THE IMPACT OF PRODUCT MANAGEMENT ON BUSINESS SUCCESS 40

CHAPTER SIX: CUSTOMER CENTRIC THINKING AND USER RESEARCH 51

CHAPTER SEVEN: STRATEGIC PLANNING AND SETTING A VISION 60

CHAPTER EIGHT: MANAGING PRODUCT ROADMAPS AND PRIORITIZATION 71

CHAPTER NINE: NAVIGATING CHALLENGES AND MAKING TOUGH DECISIONS 78

CHAPTER TEN: METRICS, DATA AND PERFORMANCE EVALUATION 92

CHAPTER ELEVEN: CAREER DEVELOPMENT AND GROWTH AS A PRODUCT MANAGER 107

CHAPTER TWELEVE: FUTURE TRENDS IN PRODUCT MANAGEMENT 115

CHAPTER THIRTEEN: FINAL THOUGHTS 125

PREFACE

Why Should I Be a Product Manager? It offers a comprehensive exploration of the dynamic role of product management, shedding light on why this career path is both compelling and impactful. The book begins with a foundational overview, detailing the essential responsibilities and daily tasks that define the role. It emphasizes how product managers are pivotal in driving innovation and business growth, demonstrating through case studies how their contributions can significantly shape a company's success.

It delves into the skills and personal qualities needed to excel as a professional, including leadership, strategic thinking, and effective communication. Readers will learn about the diverse stages of the product lifecycle and how to navigate and influence each phase to ensure successful outcomes. The discussion extends to the importance of building and leading cross-functional teams, collaborating with various departments to achieve cohesive and effective development.

We also explore the crucial aspects of customer-centric thinking and user research, highlighting how understanding and prioritizing client needs is fundamental to success. It also addresses the strategic elements of this career, including vision setting, roadmap management, and the balancing of short-term and long-term goals. Practical advice is provided on managing challenges, making tough decisions, and using data to drive performance and measure success.

Finally, the book offers insights into career development and growth within the sector, outlining pathways for advancement. It also looks ahead to future trends in the field, preparing readers to stay ahead in an evolving industry. Overall, it serves as both an introduction to the field and a compass for those considering a career in product management.

DEDICATION

To everyone who dreams of creating something extraordinary and making a real impact, this book is for you. May it inspire you to embrace the challenges, celebrate the triumphs, and find joy in every step of your journey as a product manager.

Here's to shaping the future with passion and purpose.

CHAPTER ONE

WELCOME TO PRODUCT MANAGEMENT

Product management is a dynamic and multifaceted role that sits at the intersection of business, technology, and user experience. At its core, it is about guiding a product from conception to market, ensuring it meets client needs while aligning with the company's strategic goals. This position is crucial in modern business environments, where innovation and customer-centricity are pivotal for success.

An Overview

This involves the end-to-end process of developing and delivering a product. A product manager (PM) is responsible for defining the vision, setting strategic goals, and ensuring that the product meets market demands. This role encompasses a wide range of activities, including market research, product design, development oversight, and go-to-market strategies.

For instance, developing a clear vision that aligns with the company's strategic objectives. This involves conducting market research to understand customer needs, market trends, and the competitive niche. Based on this research, they create and maintain a roadmap that outlines the development and release of features, ensuring that the solution evolves in accordance with user expectations and business goals.

It also requires cross-functional collaboration, working with engineering, marketing, and sales teams to bring the creation to market. Performance evaluation is also crucial, as it involves measuring success through metrics and customer feedback. This ongoing assessment helps refine the product and strategy, ensuring continuous alignment with both client needs and company objectives.

The role of a product manager varies by industry and company size, but the core responsibilities remain consistent: driving product success and ensuring it delivers value to both the customer and the business.

It is important to understand how this field has evolved with time. Product management, as a formal discipline, has evolved significantly over the past few decades. Originally, the role was primarily associated with consumer goods, where product managers were responsible for the entire lifecycle of a product, from market research to product development and marketing. The advent of technology and digital products brought new dimensions to the field, making it a more integral part of technology companies.

In the tech industry, it began to take shape in the 1980s with the rise of software products. Companies like Microsoft and IBM pioneered the role, focusing on software development and user experience. As technology continued to advance, the role of the product manager expanded to include responsibilities such as managing agile development processes, leveraging data analytics, and driving digital transformation. Today, product management has become a vital function in almost every industry, from healthcare to finance and beyond. The role has adapted to new challenges, including rapid technological advancements, evolving customer expectations, and the need for cross-functional teamwork.

It has significant functions in varying industries. In the tech industry, product management is pivotal in driving innovation and ensuring that software and hardware products meet user needs. Tech companies rely heavily on product managers to translate complex technical concepts into user-friendly products. They play a crucial role in defining product features, prioritizing development tasks, and overseeing the product lifecycle. For example, consider a company like Apple. Apple's product managers are responsible for defining the vision for products like the iPhone or MacBook, working closely with engineering teams to ensure that these products deliver a seamless user experience. They conduct market research to identify emerging trends and customer needs, which informs product development and marketing strategies.

A second case study is the consumer goods sector, where it focuses on developing products that appeal to customers and driving sales. Product managers in this industry work on everything from market research and product design to packaging and distribution. They must balance consumer preferences with production capabilities and cost considerations. For instance, a company like Procter & Gamble (P&G) has product managers who oversee the development of products like Tide detergent or Pampers diapers. These PMs work to ensure that their products meet consumer expectations, stay ahead of competitors, and align with the company's brand values.

Product management principles are also applied in service-oriented industries, such as healthcare and financial services. In these sectors, professionals might focus on developing new service offerings, improving customer experiences, or streamlining operations.

In a healthcare setting, for example, a product manager might work on developing a new telemedicine platform. They would need to understand regulatory requirements, patient needs, and integration with existing healthcare systems. Similarly, in financial services, a PM might oversee the development of a new mobile banking app, focusing on user experience, security features, and integration with backend systems.

There is no proper functioning without the professionals behind the scene. Here are some of their responsibilities.

Product Vision and Strategy: One of the most critical responsibilities of a product manager is to define the vision and strategy. This involves understanding market needs, identifying opportunities, and setting a clear direction for the solution. The product vision serves as a guiding light for the development team and helps align the product with the company's strategic goals. A well-defined vision should be ambitious yet achievable, providing a clear roadmap for the product's evolution. For instance, the vision for a new social media platform might be to "connect people around the world in meaningful ways," which would guide decisions related to features, user experience, and marketing.

Market Research and Analysis: This is fundamental to successful product management. Professionals must gather and analyze data to understand customer needs, market trends, and competitive dynamics. This involves conducting surveys, interviews, and focus groups, as well as analyzing industry reports and market data. For example, a PM working on a new fitness app might conduct user interviews to understand what features potential users find most valuable. They might also analyze competitor apps to identify gaps in the market and opportunities for differentiation.

Roadmap Development: Creating and managing a roadmap is another crucial responsibility. The roadmap outlines the planned development and release of product features and updates. It helps prioritize tasks, allocate resources, and communicate progress to stakeholders. A product roadmap should be dynamic, evolving as new information becomes available and market conditions change. For instance, if user feedback indicates a need for a new feature, the PM might adjust the roadmap to accommodate this request while balancing other priorities.

Cross-Functional Collaboration: They work closely with various teams within the organization, including engineering, design, marketing, and sales. They must ensure that these teams are aligned and working towards the same goals. Effective collaboration is essential for successful product development and launch. For example, during the development of a new software feature, a PM might work with the engineering team to ensure that the feature is technically feasible and with the design team to create a user-friendly interface. They would also collaborate with the marketing team to develop a go-to-market strategy and with the sales team to ensure they have the necessary information and tools to sell the product.

Performance Measurement: Measuring the success of a creation is critical for understanding its impact and making data-driven decisions. Product managers use various metrics and key performance indicators (KPIs) to assess the product's performance and identify areas for improvement. For instance, a PM might track metrics such as user engagement, customer satisfaction, and revenue growth. By analyzing this data, they can make informed decisions about future product enhancements and strategic adjustments.

To illustrate the role of product management, let's look at a few real-life examples.

Example 1: The Rise of Slack

Slack, the popular team collaboration tool, offers a compelling example of effective product management. The product was developed by Stewart Butterfield and his team, who identified a gap in the market for a better way to communicate within teams. The product managers at Slack focused on creating a user-friendly interface, integrating with other tools, and continually improving the product based on user feedback. Their efforts resulted in a highly successful product that transformed the way teams collaborate.

Example 2: The Evolution of Netflix

Netflix is another example of successful product management. The company started as a DVD rental service but evolved into a leading streaming platform. Product managers at Netflix played a key role in this transformation, focusing on improving the user experience, expanding content offerings, and leveraging data analytics to drive content recommendations. Their strategic vision and execution helped Netflix become a dominant player in the entertainment industry.

Why Product Management Might Be Right for You

This sector offers a unique blend of challenges and rewards. If you enjoy solving complex problems, working with diverse teams, and making a tangible impact, this role might be a great fit for you. Product managers have the opportunity to shape the future of products and influence the success of their organizations.

There are some factors you can consider when making this decision.

Alignment with Personal Goals: Consider how product management aligns with your career aspirations and personal goals. If you're passionate about innovation, customer experience, and strategic thinking, product management provides a platform to apply these interests in a meaningful way. The role offers a blend of creativity, analytical thinking, and leadership that can be both fulfilling and impactful.

Career Fulfillment: This field can be incredibly rewarding, offering a sense of accomplishment as you bring a product from concept to market and see it succeed. The role provides opportunities for professional growth and development, as well as the chance to work on cutting-edge projects and technologies.

Making a Difference: One of the most satisfying aspects of product management is the ability to make a difference in people's lives. Whether you're developing a new app, improving a consumer product, or creating a service, your work has the potential to impact customers and drive positive change.

Product management is an interesting field that plays a crucial part in driving innovation and ensuring business success. It involves defining a product vision, conducting market research, managing development roadmaps, collaborating with cross-functional teams, and measuring performance. With its significance across various industries and its impact on organizational success, product management offers a rewarding and dynamic career path for those who are passionate about creating value and making a difference.

As we continue through this book, we'll delve deeper into the specific aspects of product management, explore the skills and qualities needed for success, and provide practical insights to help you thrive in this exciting field. Welcome to the world of product management—where your journey to shaping the future begins.

CHAPTER TWO

UNDERSTANDING THE PRODCUT LIFECYCLE

The product lifecycle is a crucial framework that guides the journey of a product from its initial conception to its eventual phase-out. Understanding each stage of this lifecycle is essential for Product Managers (PMs) who are responsible for steering the product through these phases, ensuring its success, and maximizing its impact. This chapter explores the stages of product development and provides insights into how PMs navigate and influence each stage effectively.

Stages of Product Development

Idea Generation

The product lifecycle begins with idea generation, where new product concepts are born. This stage involves brainstorming, research, and the identification of opportunities based on market needs, emerging trends, or gaps in the current offerings. In the idea generation stage, several key activities are essential for cultivating new product concepts. Market research plays a crucial role, involving the conduct of surveys, interviews, and competitive analysis to gather valuable insights about customer needs, market trends, and potential opportunities.

Additionally, leveraging existing customer feedback and suggestions helps identify areas where current offers may fall short or where new needs may emerge. Internal brainstorming sessions are equally important, as they bring together diverse perspectives from across the organization. These collaborative efforts help in generating and refining ideas, ensuring that they are not only innovative but also feasible and aligned with the company's strategic goals.

Product Managers play a pivotal role in filtering and prioritizing ideas at this stage. They assess the feasibility, potential market impact, and alignment with strategic goals. PMs often use frameworks such as SWOT analysis (Strengths, Weaknesses, Opportunities, and Threats) to evaluate ideas and decide which ones warrant further exploration.

Concept Development and Testing

Once a viable idea is selected, it moves into the concept development stage. Here, detailed product concepts are created, and initial prototypes may be developed. This stage involves refining the product idea and testing it to validate its feasibility and desirability.

In the concept development and testing stage, several key activities are critical for refining and validating a product idea. Concept design involves creating detailed descriptions and specifications of the product, outlining its features, functionalities, and intended user experience. This is followed by prototyping, where initial versions or mock-ups of the product are developed to visualize and test the concept in a tangible form. Prototypes help in identifying potential design and functionality issues early on. Finally, concept testing involves gathering feedback from potential users or stakeholders to evaluate their reactions and perceptions of the product. This feedback is invaluable for refining the concept, making necessary adjustments, and ensuring that the product aligns with user needs and expectations before moving forward.

PMs coordinate the development of prototypes and oversee concept testing. They ensure that feedback is collected systematically and used to make informed decisions about the product's direction. PMs also work closely with designers and engineers to translate concepts into tangible prototypes.

Business Analysis

This stage involves a thorough analysis of the product's business potential. PMs assess the market opportunity, financial feasibility, and overall business impact. This analysis helps in making informed decisions about moving forward with the product development.

During the business analysis stage, several key activities are crucial for assessing a product's viability. Market analysis involves evaluating the market size, growth potential, and competitive landscape to understand the product's position and potential within the industry. This includes identifying target demographics and estimating market demand. Cost and revenue estimation follows, where development costs are calculated, pricing strategies are determined, and potential revenue streams are forecasted. This financial assessment helps gauge the product's profitability and financial feasibility. Additionally, risk assessment plays a vital role in identifying and mitigating potential risks associated with the product. This involves analyzing factors that could impact the product's success, such as market fluctuations, technical challenges, or competitive threats, and developing strategies to address these risks effectively.

PMs are responsible for conducting or overseeing the business analysis. They collaborate with finance and marketing teams to develop financial models, forecast revenue, and identify risks. The insights gained from this analysis help in securing stakeholder buy-in and determining the product's viability.

Product Development

In the product development stage, the concept is turned into a fully functional product. This phase involves detailed design, engineering, and iterative testing to ensure the product meets quality standards and user expectations.

During this stage, a series of essential activities are undertaken to bring the product from concept to reality. The process starts with the design and engineering phase, where detailed specifications and design elements are crafted to define the product's functionality and appearance. This is followed by the development phase, in which the product is built and coded according to these specifications, turning the design into a tangible prototype. Rigorous testing is then performed to uncover and resolve any issues, ensuring that the product meets quality standards and functions as intended. This methodical approach is crucial for refining the product and addressing any technical challenges before it progresses further.

Product Managers oversee the development process, ensuring that timelines, budgets, and quality standards are met. They facilitate communication between cross-functional teams, resolve any issues that arise, and ensure that the product development aligns with the initial vision and goals.

Market Testing

Before a full-scale launch, the product undergoes market testing to gauge its acceptance and performance in real-world conditions. This stage involves releasing the product to a limited audience to collect feedback and make final adjustments.

During the market testing phase, several key activities are carried out to refine the product before its full-scale release. The process begins with a pilot launch, where the product is introduced to a small, controlled group of users to gauge its performance in real-world conditions. Following this, feedback collection is crucial; insights and opinions are gathered from the test audience to pinpoint areas that may need improvement. Based on this feedback and the results of the pilot launch, necessary adjustments are made to address any identified issues and enhance the product's overall effectiveness and user experience. This iterative approach ensures that the final product is well-tuned to meet user expectations and market demands.

PMs coordinate market testing activities, ensuring that feedback is collected effectively and used to refine the product. They analyze test results and work with development teams to implement improvements. PMs also manage communication with the test audience and stakeholders.

Launch

The launch stage involves introducing the product to the broader market. This phase includes finalizing marketing strategies, preparing for distribution, and executing the product launch plan.

At the launch phase, several key activities are crucial to the product's successful introduction to the market. Marketing and promotion are central to this phase, involving the development and execution of campaigns designed to create awareness and generate demand. Ensuring effective distribution is also critical, as it involves making the product available through the right channels to reach the target audience. Coordinating the official release involves meticulous planning and execution of the event or release strategy, ensuring that all elements are in place for a smooth and impactful market entry.

Product Managers oversee the launch process, coordinating efforts across marketing, sales, and distribution teams. They ensure that all launch activities are executed as planned and that the product is successfully introduced onto the market. PMs also monitor early performance metrics and adjust strategies as needed.

Post-Launch Evaluation

After the product is launched, it is crucial to evaluate its performance and gather insights into future improvements. This stage involves monitoring the product's success, addressing any issues, and planning for future enhancements.

Following the product's launch, several key activities are essential for sustaining its success. Performance monitoring involves tracking key metrics such as sales, user engagement, and customer satisfaction to assess the product's market impact. Providing customer support is crucial, as it addresses any issues or feedback from users to ensure a positive experience. Continuous improvement is also important, focusing on identifying opportunities for product enhancements and updates based on performance data and user insights. This ongoing process helps maintain the product's relevance and effectiveness, ensuring it continues to meet user needs and expectations.

PMs are responsible for monitoring the product's performance and gathering feedback from users. They analyze data to assess the product's success and identify areas for improvement. PMs work with cross-functional teams to implement updates and ensure that the product remains competitive and meets user needs.

Product Retirement

Eventually, every product reaches the end of its lifecycle. The retirement stage involves phasing out the product, managing its discontinuation, and transitioning users to new solutions if necessary.

In the end-of-life phase, several key activities are crucial for managing the product's discontinuation. End-of-life planning involves developing a strategy for phasing out the product, which includes communicating effectively with stakeholders to ensure they are informed of the transition. Customer transition is an important aspect of this process, where efforts are made to assist customers in moving to alternative products or solutions that meet their needs. It is essential to stop production, sales, and support the item, completing the withdrawal process and ensuring a smooth conclusion to its market presence.

Product Managers oversee the retirement process, ensuring that it is executed smoothly and with minimal disruption to customers. They manage communications with users and stakeholders, handle any remaining inventory or support issues, and gather insights into future product development.

Understanding the product lifecycle is essential for Product Managers who are responsible for guiding a product from conception to retirement. Each stage of the lifecycle presents unique challenges and opportunities, and professionals play a crucial role in navigating and influencing these stages.

CHAPTER THREE

SKILLS AND QUALITIES OF A PRODUCT MANAGER

Success in this field requires more than just technical knowledge or a keen market sense. It demands a blend of essential skills and personal qualities that enable PMs to navigate complex challenges, align diverse teams, and drive innovation.

Effective product managers are adept at steering their projects through uncertainty, balancing stakeholder needs, and ensuring that every aspect of the product development process contributes to its success. They embody qualities such as empathy, resilience, curiosity, and visionary thinking, which empower them to understand user needs, overcome obstacles, and anticipate future trends.

This chapter explores the crucial skills and personal attributes that distinguish top product managers. By mastering these qualities, PMs can enhance their ability to lead, innovate, and ultimately deliver exceptional products.

Essential Skill

Communication: Effective product managers excel in both verbal and written communication. They must articulate the vision, strategy, and product requirements clearly to diverse stakeholders, including engineers, designers, marketers, and executives. This involves not just conveying information but also listening actively to feedback and concerns. Imagine you're leading a project to develop a new feature for your product. To ensure the team understands the feature requirements, you organize a series of meetings with different stakeholders such as engineers, designers, and marketing personnel. You create a detailed document outlining the feature's specifications and goals and share it with the team. During the meetings, you clearly articulate the user needs and the expected outcomes while actively listening to the team's feedback and addressing their concerns. This clear and effective communication ensures everyone is aligned and knows their responsibilities.

Leadership: Leadership in product management is not about authority but about influence. Product managers must inspire and guide cross-functional teams, foster collaboration, and ensure alignment with the product vision. They should also be adept at decision-making and managing conflicts within the team. Your team faces a significant technical challenge that could delay the product launch. As the product manager, you step up to lead the charge. You call a meeting with the development team to discuss the issue, listen to their input, and facilitate brainstorming sessions to explore possible solutions. You encourage team members to voice their ideas and provide support for the chosen solution. By fostering collaboration and motivating the team, you guide them through the problem-solving process and help them stay focused on the goal.

Problem-Solving: The ability to tackle complex issues and find effective solutions is crucial. Product managers face a myriad of challenges, from technical constraints to market competition. They must use analytical skills to dissect problems and creative thinking to generate innovative solutions. An example is you receive feedback from users that a critical feature in your app is too complex and difficult to use. To address this, you initiate a root-cause analysis by reviewing user feedback, conducting usability tests, and examining usage data. Based on your findings, you identify that the feature's user interface is cluttered. You collaborated with the design team to simplify the interface and conduct further testing to ensure the changes improve usability. Your problem-solving approach results in a more intuitive user experience and higher user satisfaction.

Analytical Thinking: Professionals need to be data-driven, capable of interpreting metrics, analyzing market trends, and making informed decisions based on quantitative and qualitative data. Analytical thinking helps in understanding customer needs, tracking product performance, and optimizing strategies. For instance, your company is considering adding a new feature to its product but needs to evaluate its potential impact. You analyze customer data, market trends, and competitive offers to assess demand. You use data analysis tools to model potential outcomes and project the feature's impact on user engagement and revenue. After presenting your findings to the stakeholders, you provide data-driven recommendations on whether to proceed with the feature, helping to make an informed decision.

Prioritization: With limited resources and competing demands, prioritization is key. Product managers must assess which features or improvements will deliver the most value and align with strategic goals. They need to balance short-term needs with long-term vision and make tough trade-offs. In a situation where you are managing a backlog of feature requests and bug fixes, and the team's capacity is limited. To prioritize effectively, you use the MoSCoW method to categorize items into Must-have, Should-have, Could-have, and Won't-have for this release. You collaborate with stakeholders to assess the value and urgency of each item and make trade-offs based on the impact on the product's overall goals and user needs. This structured approach ensures that the most important tasks are addressed first, and resources are allocated efficiently.

Technical Understanding: While not necessarily engineers, effective product managers should have a solid grasp of the technical aspects of their product. This helps in communicating effectively with development teams, understanding the feasibility of proposed solutions, and managing technical debt. During the development of a new feature, the engineering team encounters a technical limitation related to scalability. Although you're not a developer, you take the initiative to learn about the technical constraints and engage in discussions with the engineering team to understand the issue. You research potential solutions and work with the team to find an approach that balances technical feasibility with user needs. Your technical understanding helps bridge the gap between engineering and product management, leading to a successful implementation of the feature.

Customer Focus: A deep understanding of customer needs and pain points is essential. Product managers should engage with users to gather feedback, validate ideas, and ensure that the product delivers genuine value. A customer-centric approach drives meaningful innovation and improves user satisfaction. When you notice a decline in user engagement with one of your product's features. To understand the cause, you may set up user interviews and conduct surveys to gather feedback directly from the customers. You analyze the responses and identify that users find the feature confusing and hard to navigate. Based on this feedback, you work with the design team to simplify the user interface and improve the feature's usability. By addressing the specific concerns of users, you enhance the feature's effectiveness and improve overall customer satisfaction.

Personal Qualities for Success

Empathy: Empathy enables product managers to connect with users and team members on a deeper level. By understanding and sharing the feelings of others, they can better address user needs and foster a positive, collaborative team environment.

Resilience: The role of a product manager involves navigating setbacks and maintaining motivation despite challenges. Resilience helps in overcoming obstacles, adapting to changes, and persisting through difficult phases of product development.

Curiosity: A strong sense of curiosity drives continuous learning and improvement. Product managers should be eager to explore new technologies, understand industry trends, and seek out innovative approaches. Curiosity fuels growth and helps in staying ahead of the competition.

Visionary Thinking: Effective product managers possess a forward-thinking mindset. They should be able to envision the future of their product and industry, set ambitious goals, and inspire their team with a clear and compelling vision.

Decisiveness: Product management often requires making swift and informed decisions. Decisiveness involves weighing options, evaluating risks, and taking action confidently, even when faced with uncertainty.

Adaptability: The ability to adjust strategies and approaches in response to changing circumstances is vital. Adaptability ensures that product managers can pivot, when necessary, embrace new opportunities, and handle evolving market conditions.

Accountability: Taking ownership of decisions and their outcomes is the hallmark of a great product manager. Accountability involves accepting responsibility for both successes and failures and learning from experiences to drive future improvements.

How Professionals Can Imbibe These Skills and Qualities

It is one thing to have theoretical knowledge and another to know how to apply it practically. We will look at some tips to apply these skills and qualities to our work activities effectively.

Developing Communication Skills: Engage in active listening exercises to improve your ability to understand and respond to others effectively. You can also regularly request feedback on your communication style and work on areas of improvement.

Cultivating Leadership: Learn to volunteer to lead smaller projects or teams to build your leadership skills in a low-risk environment. Seek mentorship from experienced leaders to learn about effective leadership practices.

Enhancing Problem-Solving Abilities: Participate in or organize brainstorming sessions to practice creative problem-solving. This helps in creating new ideas and refining existing projects. Study case studies of successful and failed products to understand different approaches to problem-solving.

Strengthening Analytical Skills: Familiarize yourself with data analysis tools and techniques, such as Excel, SQL, or data visualization software. These tools can be used to improve your output as technology becomes part of our daily activities in this current dispensation. Enroll in courses on data analysis and interpretation to build a solid analytical foundation.

Improving Prioritization: Implement frameworks like the Eisenhower Matrix or Moscow method to practice prioritizing tasks effectively. Regularly reflect on past decisions to understand your prioritization process and make improvements.

Building Technical Understanding: Consider learning the basics of coding or software development to enhance your technical understanding. It is also imperative to learn how to collaborate closely with engineers to gain insights into technical aspects and challenges.

Fostering Customer Focus: Engage in user research activities, such as interviews and surveys, consistently to understand customer needs. Observe and participate in usability testing to gain direct insights into user experiences and pain points. This will aid in being updated on client preferences and trends.

Embracing Empathy: Participate in exercises designed to enhance empathy, such as role-playing or perspective-taking activities. Actively seek and incorporate user feedback to better understand and address their needs.

Building Resilience: Engage in stress management techniques, such as mindfulness or exercise, to build resilience. Analyze past setbacks and develop strategies for overcoming similar challenges in the future.

Nurturing Curiosity: Read industry blogs, attend webinars, and participate in conferences to stay curious about new developments. Regularly experiment with new ideas and approaches to fuel your curiosity and innovation.

Developing Visionary Thinking: Work on setting and pursuing long-term goals to enhance your visionary thinking. Participate in strategic planning sessions to practice envisioning future scenarios and outcomes.

Enhancing Decisiveness: Practice making small decisions quickly to build your confidence and decisiveness. Reflect on your decision-making processes to identify and address any areas for improvement. The goal is to get better and improve on the existing decision-making process.

Building Adaptability: Actively seek out opportunities to work in dynamic environments to build your adaptability. Practice adjusting your plans and approaches in response to changing circumstances.

Fostering Accountability: Embrace ownership of your projects and their outcomes and be transparent about your actions and decisions. Continuously seek feedback on your performance and take responsibility for addressing areas of improvement.

By actively working on these skills and qualities, interested enthusiasts can work their character portfolio in achieving their goal of working in the industry. It is also beneficial to professionals, who can enhance their effectiveness as product managers and drive greater success in their roles.

CHAPTER FOUR

BUILDING AND LEADING CROSS-FUCTIONAL TEAMS

Building and leading cross-functional teams is a cornerstone of effective product management. It's not just about assembling a group of talented individuals but about strategically aligning diverse skill sets, fostering collaboration, and steering the team towards a unified goal. This chapter delves into how product managers can select the right cross-functional teams and ensure they work harmoniously to bring a successful product to the market.

Selecting the Right Cross-Functional Team

Choosing the right cross-functional team is crucial for the success of a product. This involves not only identifying the right mix of skills but also understanding how each team member's role and expertise will contribute to the product's development. Here's how product managers can make informed decisions about team composition.

Before selecting a team, it's essential to have a clear understanding of the product requirements. This includes defining the product vision, goals, and key features. By having a well-articulated vision, product managers can identify the specific skills and expertise needed. For instance, if the product requires advanced technical features, including engineers with specific technical skills becomes crucial. Conversely, if market penetration is a primary goal, marketing and sales experts with industry-specific knowledge will be vital.

Assessing the skill sets and expertise of potential team members is crucial. Look for individuals with a track record of relevant experience and a deep understanding of their respective fields. For example, when selecting engineers, consider their experience with similar technologies or products. When choosing marketing professionals, evaluate their success in launching similar solutions or reaching similar target audiences. Beyond individual skills, the ability of team members to collaborate effectively is critical. Assess potential team members for their ability to work well in a team environment, communicate clearly, and adapt to different working styles. Team dynamics can significantly influence productivity and morale. For instance, a team composed of highly specialized individuals who are not accustomed to collaborative work may face challenges in communication and coordination.

A diverse team brings varied perspectives and ideas, which can lead to more innovative solutions and a more comprehensive understanding of the market. When assembling a cross-functional team, consider including members from different backgrounds, experiences, and disciplines. Diversity fosters creativity and can help address challenges from multiple angles, enhancing the overall quality of the initiative. Ensure that the team members not only have the right skills but also align with the organization's goals and culture. A team that resonates with the company's values and mission is more likely to be engaged and motivated. This alignment helps in creating a cohesive team where everyone is working towards a common goal and is committed to the product's success.

When selecting members for a cross-functional team, it's valuable to consider their previous collaboration experiences and team chemistry. Individuals who have worked together effectively in the past can bring established dynamics and mutual understanding to the new project, which can enhance team cohesion and productivity. For example, if a previous project team demonstrated a strong ability to collaborate and deliver results, incorporating those same members into the new team can leverage their proven synergy. This prior experience can reduce the time needed for team members to acclimate to one another, facilitating smoother interactions and more efficient problem-solving. Additionally, considering how well potential team members mesh with each other on a personal and professional level can prevent interpersonal conflicts and foster a more harmonious working environment.

Assessing the availability and commitment levels of potential team members is another crucial factor in selecting the right cross-functional team. It's essential to understand each candidate's current workload, availability, and willingness to commit time and effort to the new project. A team member who is already stretched thin with other responsibilities might struggle to dedicate the necessary focus and energy, potentially impacting the project's progress and quality. Conversely, individuals who demonstrate strong commitment and a clear alignment with the project's goals are likely to contribute more effectively. Evaluating this aspect ensures that the team can operate at full capacity without overburdening any single member, thereby maintaining a balanced and productive work environment.

Techniques for Effective Team Leadership and Coordination

Leading a cross-functional team requires more than just managing tasks; it involves inspiring, guiding, and ensuring effective coordination among diverse team members. Here are techniques for effective leadership and coordination:

Establish Clear Roles and Responsibilities: Clearly define each team member's role and responsibilities to avoid overlap and confusion. Everyone should understand their specific tasks, how they contribute to the overall product, and how their work intersects with others. Creating detailed role descriptions and a

RACI (Responsible, Accountable, Consulted, and Informed) matrix can help clarify these aspects.

Foster Open Communication: Open communication is key to successful collaboration. Create channels for regular updates, feedback, and discussion. Utilize tools such as project management software, chat platforms, and regular meetings to facilitate communication. Encourage team members to share their insights, concerns, and suggestions openly, and ensure that there is a structured process for addressing issues that arise.

Implement Agile Methodologies: Agile methodologies, such as Scrum or Kanban, can greatly enhance team coordination and flexibility. Agile practices emphasize iterative development, regular feedback, and adaptive planning. By adopting Agile methodologies, product managers can ensure that the team remains aligned, responds to changes effectively, and continuously improves the product through incremental progress.

Promote a Collaborative Culture: Build a culture of collaboration by encouraging team members to work together, share knowledge, and support one another. Facilitate cross-functional workshops, brainstorming sessions, and collaborative problem-solving activities. Recognize and celebrate collaborative efforts and achievements to reinforce the value of teamwork.

Set Clear Goals and Milestones: Define clear, measurable goals and milestones for the team. This helps in tracking progress, maintaining focus, and ensuring that everyone is working towards the same objectives. Regularly review progress against these goals and make adjustments as necessary. Celebrate milestones to maintain motivation and momentum.

Provide Resources and Support: Ensure that the team has access to the necessary resources, tools, and support to perform their tasks effectively. This includes providing training, access to relevant information, and removing any obstacles that may hinder progress. By addressing these needs, product managers can enable the team to work more efficiently and achieve better results.

Encourage Continuous Learning and Improvement: Foster an environment where continuous learning and improvement are valued. Encourage team members to seek out learning opportunities, attend industry conferences, and stay updated with the latest trends and technologies. Regularly review processes and practices to identify areas for improvement and implement changes to enhance team performance.

Integrating Cross-Functional Teams into Product Development

Once the right team is in place, integrating them into the product development process effectively is crucial. Let us examine how to ensure that the team functions cohesively and contributes to the product's success.

Ensure that all team members have a shared understanding of the product vision and goals. This shared vision helps align individual efforts and fosters a sense of purpose. Regularly communicate the product's objectives and how each team member's work contributes to achieving them. Effective coordination across functions is essential for seamless product development. Facilitate regular cross-functional meetings to ensure that all departments are aligned and informed. This helps in identifying dependencies, addressing potential conflicts, and ensuring that everyone is on the same page.

Conflicts and differences of opinion are natural in cross-functional teams. Address these conflicts constructively by encouraging open dialogue and seeking common ground. Mediate disagreements by focusing on the product's goals and finding solutions that align with the team's objectives. Continuously monitor the team's progress and the effectiveness of processes. Gather feedback from team members and stakeholders to identify areas for improvement. Be prepared to make adjustments to processes, roles, or communication methods as needed to enhance team performance and product development.

Recognize and celebrate the team's successes to build morale and reinforce positive behaviors. Similarly, learn from failures and setbacks by conducting post-mortem analyses to understand what went wrong and how to avoid similar issues in the future. Use these insights to improve future projects and enhance team performance.

Managing Stakeholder Expectations and Engagement

This is crucial for ensuring that cross-functional teams are aligned with broader organizational goals and that their work meets stakeholder expectations. Stakeholders can include internal executives, external customers, partners, and other entities that have a vested interest in the product's outcome. Understanding and addressing their needs and concerns can significantly impact the project's success and the team's effectiveness. Product managers can effectively manage stakeholder expectations and engagement through the following ways:

Identify Key Stakeholders: Begin by identifying all relevant stakeholders involved in or affected by the product. This includes internal stakeholders such as senior management, department heads, and other teams, as well as external stakeholders like customers, partners, and industry regulators. Understanding who the stakeholders are and their level of influence and interest in the product will help tailor engagement strategies to meet their specific needs.

Understand Stakeholder Needs and Expectations: Engage with stakeholders early in the product development process to understand their needs, expectations, and concerns. Conduct interviews, surveys, and workshops to gather their input and ensure that their perspectives are considered. This will help in aligning the product's features and goals with stakeholder expectations and identifying potential areas of conflict or concern early on.

Establish Clear Communication Channels: Develop clear and effective communication channels to keep stakeholders informed and engaged throughout the product development lifecycle. Regular updates, progress reports, and feedback sessions are essential for maintaining transparency and managing expectations. Utilize various communication tools and methods, such as newsletters, meetings, and collaborative platforms, to ensure that stakeholders receive timely and relevant information.

Set Realistic Expectations: Clearly communicate what can and cannot be achieved within the project's scope, timeline, and budget. Setting realistic expectations helps manage stakeholder satisfaction and prevents potential disappointments. It's important to be transparent about any limitations or constraints and to provide alternative solutions or adjustments where necessary.

Involve Stakeholders in Key Decisions: Involve stakeholders in critical decision-making processes to ensure their input is considered and to gain their buy-in. This collaborative approach not only helps in aligning the product with stakeholder expectations but also fosters a sense of ownership and commitment among stakeholders. Regularly seek feedback and be prepared to make adjustments based on their insights.

Address Concerns and Resolve Conflicts: Actively address any concerns or conflicts that arise with stakeholders. Implement a structured approach for managing and resolving issues, including identifying the root cause, discussing potential solutions, and negotiating compromises. Prompt and effective resolution of conflicts helps maintain positive relationships and keeps the project on track.

Monitor and Evaluate Stakeholder Satisfaction: Continuously monitor and evaluate stakeholder satisfaction throughout the product development process. Use surveys, feedback sessions, and performance metrics to assess how well stakeholder needs are being met. Regularly review this feedback to make necessary adjustments and improvements to the product and the engagement strategy.

Celebrate Successes and Communicate Achievements: Recognize and celebrate milestones and achievements with stakeholders. Effective communication of successes not only reinforces positive relationships but also builds credibility and trust. Share key accomplishments, success stories, and the impact of the product to highlight the value and benefits delivered.

Building and leading cross-functional teams is an interesting and multifaceted aspect of product management. By carefully selecting team members, implementing effective leadership techniques, and integrating the team into the product development process, product managers can drive successful outcomes and create products that meet market needs and exceed expectations. Balancing diverse skill sets, fostering collaboration, and aligning the team with a shared vision are key to achieving product success and maintaining a motivated and effective team.

CHAPTER FIVE

THE IMPACT OF PRODUCT MANAGEMENT ON BUSINESS SUCCESS

Product management is a critical function within any organization, shaping how businesses innovate, compete, and thrive. This chapter delves into the divergent role of product management, examining how product managers drive innovation, fuel business growth, and contribute to overall success. By analyzing case studies and discussing key strategies, best practices, and emerging trends, this chapter provides a comprehensive look at the impact of product management.

How Product Managers Drive Innovation and Business Growth

Product managers are pivotal in steering innovation and driving business growth. They serve as the bridge between market needs and company capabilities, ensuring that products not only meet current demands but also anticipate future trends.

Product managers conduct extensive market research to identify unmet needs and emerging opportunities. This involves analyzing market trends, customer feedback, and competitive landscape. By understanding the gaps in the market, managers can propose innovative solutions that align with strategic business goals. Innovation often requires collaboration across various departments such as engineering, design, marketing, and sales. Product managers lead these cross-functional teams, ensuring that each department's efforts are synchronized toward achieving a common goal. Their ability to communicate effectively and align diverse perspectives is crucial for successful product development.

Agile methodologies are instrumental in fostering innovation. Product managers utilize agile frameworks like Scrum or Kanban to facilitate iterative development, allowing teams to quickly adapt to changes and incorporate feedback. This iterative approach helps in refining products based on real-time insights and ensures that the final product meets market demands. These professionals are responsible for setting key performance indicators (KPIs) and measuring the success of product initiatives. By analyzing metrics such as user engagement, revenue growth, and customer satisfaction, they can assess the impact of their strategies and make data-driven decisions for continuous improvement.

Case Studies of Successful Product Management

Examining real-world examples of successful product management can provide valuable insights into the best practices and strategies that drive business success.

Case Study 1: Apple's iPhone

Apple's launch of the iPhone is a prime example of effective product management. By integrating brilliant technology with user-centric design, Apple revolutionized the smartphone industry. Product managers at Apple identified a gap in the market for a versatile, intuitive device and led the development of a product that combined a phone, an iPod, and an internet communicator into one. The iPhone's success demonstrated the power of visionary product management in driving innovation and establishing market leadership.

Case Study 2: Netflix's Streaming Service

Netflix's transition from DVD rentals to a streaming service highlights the impact of strategic product process. By recognizing the shift in consumer behavior towards digital content consumption, Netflix's product managers spearheaded the development of a user-friendly streaming platform. This strategic pivot allowed Netflix to dominate the streaming market and expand its global subscriber base.

Case Study 3: Tesla's Electric Vehicles

Tesla's success in the electric vehicle (EV) market is a testament to effective product management in a highly competitive industry. Tesla's product managers focused on delivering high-performance, aesthetically appealing electric cars with a robust charging infrastructure. Their ability to innovate and address both customer and market needs has positioned Tesla as a leader in the EV space.

Case Study 4: Airbnb's Platform Evolution

Airbnb's evolution from a simple room-sharing website to a comprehensive travel platform showcases the role of product management in scaling a business. Product managers at The Company continuously enhanced the platform by introducing new features, improving user experience, and expanding into new markets. This strategic management of product evolution has been crucial in its global expansion and success.

To drive business success, product managers must employ strategic approaches tailored to their company's goals and market conditions. A clear vision provides direction and purpose for product development efforts. Product managers must articulate a compelling vision that aligns with the company's overall strategy and resonates with target customers. This vision serves as a guiding principle for decision-making and prioritization. Effective product management involves prioritizing features based on customer needs, business value, and technical feasibility. Product managers use frameworks like the MoSCoW method (Must have, should have, could have, Won't have) to prioritize features and create a product roadmap that balances short-term objectives with long-term goals.

Customer engagement is crucial for developing products that meet market demands. Product managers should establish channels for collecting customer feedback, such as surveys, focus groups, and usability testing. Incorporating this feedback into the product development process helps ensure that the final product delivers value and addresses user needs. The business environment is dynamic, and product managers must be agile in responding to market changes. This involves staying informed about industry trends, competitive actions, and evolving customer preferences. Product managers should be prepared to adjust strategies and pivot when necessary to maintain relevance and achieve success.

Challenges Faced by Product Managers and How to Overcome Them

Product management is not without its challenges. Understanding these challenges and developing strategies to address them is essential for success.

Balancing Short-Term and Long-Term Goals: Product managers often face the challenge of balancing immediate deliverables with long-term strategic objectives. To address this, they should prioritize initiatives based on their impact and align them with the overall product vision. Effective time management and stakeholder communication are key to achieving this balance.

Managing Cross-Functional Team Dynamics: Leading cross-functional teams can be challenging due to differing perspectives and priorities. Product managers should foster a collaborative environment by setting clear goals, facilitating open communication, and addressing conflicts promptly. Building strong relationships with team members and stakeholders helps ensure smooth collaboration.

Navigating Resource Constraints: Resource limitations can impact product development timelines and quality. Product managers must be adept at resource planning and prioritization to maximize efficiency. This may involve negotiating with stakeholders, optimizing processes, and making informed trade-offs to achieve the best possible outcomes within available resources.

Handling Uncertainty and Risk: Product development often involves uncertainty and risk. Product managers should adopt risk management practices, such as conducting thorough market research, running pilot tests, and developing contingency plans. Being proactive in identifying potential risks and having strategies in place to mitigate them can help navigate uncertainties effectively.

Navigating Organizational Politics and Bureaucracy: Product managers often encounter organizational politics and bureaucracy, which can hinder decision-making and slow down product development. Navigating these internal dynamics while trying to push forward product initiatives can be frustrating and counterproductive. To effectively manage organizational politics and bureaucracy, product managers should focus on building alliances and influencing key stakeholders. Developing relationships with influential figures within the company can provide support for your initiatives and help you maneuver through bureaucratic obstacles more smoothly. Strategic communication is also crucial; by aligning your product goals with organizational priorities and addressing the concerns of various stakeholders, you can facilitate smoother approvals and garner support. Additionally, understanding the internal processes and decision-making structures of the organization is vital. This knowledge allows you to anticipate potential roadblocks and work within the system more effectively, thus minimizing friction and accelerating progress.

Addressing Divergent Customer Needs and Expectations: Professionals often face the challenge of addressing diverse and sometimes conflicting customer needs and expectations. Balancing these varying demands while maintaining a cohesive product vision can be difficult. One effective approach to managing divergent customer needs is to segment your market into distinct groups based on shared characteristics or needs. This segmentation enables you to tailor features and solutions to different customer groups, ensuring that the most critical requirements of each segment are addressed. Prioritizing customer needs is another key strategy; using frameworks like the Kano Model can help you focus on features that offer the highest value and address the most pressing pain points. Moreover, engaging in continuous feedback by implementing mechanisms for ongoing customer input ensures that your product remains relevant and adapts to changing expectations. Regular updates based on this feedback help in meeting diverse customer needs while maintaining a unified product vision.

Aligning Product Strategy with Business Objectives: Ensuring that the product strategy aligns with broader business objectives can be challenging, especially when dealing with evolving market conditions and shifting company priorities. To maintain alignment between product strategy and business objectives, product managers should conduct regular strategy reviews. These reviews help ensure that the product roadmap remains in sync with business goals, allowing for adjustments in response to changes in priorities or market dynamics. Establishing clear key performance indicators (KPIs) that connect product outcomes with business objectives is also essential. This alignment helps in measuring the impact of your product initiatives on overall business success and justifying resource allocation. Furthermore, collaborating with executive leadership and other key decision-makers provides valuable insights into business objectives. Regular communication about how your product strategy supports these goals, combined with seeking input from leadership, ensures that your product initiatives are aligned with broader business priorities.

The field of product management is continually evolving, influenced by technological advancements and changing market dynamics. Understanding future trends can help product managers stay ahead and drive continued business success. Data analytics and artificial intelligence (AI) are transforming product management. Product managers will increasingly rely on data-driven insights to make informed decisions, predict market trends, and personalize customer experiences. Embracing data analytics tools and techniques will be essential for staying competitive.

As customer expectations rise, product experts will need to focus more on delivering exceptional customer experiences. Personalization, user-centric design, and seamless interactions will become central to product development strategies. Leveraging customer feedback and behavior data will be key to creating tailored experiences. Emerging technologies such as blockchain, augmented reality (AR), and virtual reality (VR) are shaping the future of product management. Product managers will need to explore how these technologies can enhance their products and create new value propositions. Staying informed about technological advancements will be crucial for innovation. The role of product managers is expanding to include responsibilities such as strategic planning, business development, and leadership. Product managers will need to develop a broader skill set, including strategic thinking, financial acumen, and leadership abilities. Continuous learning and adaptation will be essential for success in the evolving landscape.

Adopting the best practices can enhance the effectiveness of product management efforts and contribute to business success. Let us see certain measures you can take to incorporate this.

Building Strong Relationships with Stakeholders: Establishing and maintaining strong relationships with stakeholders is crucial for successful product management. Product managers should engage with stakeholders regularly, communicate progress, and address concerns. Building trust and aligning expectations with stakeholders helps ensure support for product initiatives.

Emphasizing Continuous Learning and Improvement: Individuals should embrace a mindset of continuous learning and improvement. This involves staying updated on industry trends, seeking feedback, and reflecting on past experiences. By continuously enhancing their skills and knowledge, product managers can adapt to changing conditions and drive better outcomes.

Leveraging Effective Communication: Clear and effective communication is vital for product managers. They must be able to articulate product vision, priorities, and progress to various audiences, including team members, executives, and customers. Developing strong communication skills helps facilitate collaboration, manage expectations, and drive successful outcomes.

Utilizing Effective Product Management Tools: Product Management Tools can streamline processes and enhance productivity. Tools for project management, customer feedback, analytics, and collaboration can aid product managers in executing their responsibilities efficiently. Evaluating and selecting the right tools based on the team's needs can significantly impact product management success.

There is no doubt that the field has a tremendous impact on business growth and success. Its influence also extends to other industries. Having a proper view of this impact is imperative in growing and refining your skill as a professional. It is an essential tool to have in one's arsenal.

CHAPTER SIX

CUSTOMER CENTRIC THINKING AND USER RESEARCH

In today's fast-paced, competitive business environment, understanding and prioritizing customer needs is more critical than ever. The ability to incorporate user feedback into the product development process not only sets apart successful products but also defines the role of an exceptional product manager. This chapter explores the foundational methods for understanding customer needs, emphasizes the importance of user research, and outlines how to effectively integrate user feedback into the product development cycle.

The Essence of Customer-Centric Thinking

Customer-centric thinking is the philosophy of placing the customer at the core of your product strategy and decision-making process. It goes beyond traditional market research to deeply understand the behaviors, preferences, and pain points of your target audience. This approach ensures that the product not only meets but exceeds customer expectations, leading to higher satisfaction, loyalty, and ultimately, business success.

There are importance of customer-centric thinking being incorporated into your processes. Some of them include:

1. Informed Decision-Making: Customer-centric thinking ensures that product decisions are based on real customer needs rather than assumptions. This reduces the risk of product failures and increases the likelihood of market success.

2. Enhanced User Experience: By focusing on the customer's perspective, product managers can design features and experiences that are intuitive and valuable, leading to a better user experience.

3. Competitive Advantage: Companies that effectively understand and address customer needs often outpace competitors who rely solely on internal opinions or trends.

4. Customer Loyalty and Retention: Products that genuinely solve customer problems build trust and loyalty, fostering long-term relationships and repeat business.

We will be looking at several methods for understanding and prioritizing customer needs. **First** is **customer interviews.** Customer interviews are a qualitative research method that provides deep insights into user motivations, behaviors, and pain points. Conducting structured or semi-structured interviews allows product managers to gather detailed information about how users interact with a product and what they desire from it. To conduct effective customer interviews, start by preparing a detailed discussion guide. This guide should outline a set of open-ended questions and topics designed to explore various aspects of the user's experience. Open-ended questions encourage detailed, qualitative responses, allowing you to gain deeper insights into the participants' perspectives and needs. Next, focus on building a report with the interviewees. Creating a comfortable and welcoming environment helps participants feel at ease, which can lead to more honest and insightful feedback. Establishing a connection and making participants feel valued can significantly enhance the quality of the information you gather. After the interviews, it is crucial to analyze the collected data thoroughly. Identify common themes and patterns across the responses to uncover overarching customer needs and pain points. This thematic analysis helps to distill complex feedback into actionable insights, guiding product improvements and strategic decisions.

A **second method** is using **surveys and questionnaires**. Surveys are a quantitative research tool used to gather data from a large number of users quickly. They are effective for validating assumptions and quantifying customer preferences. When designing surveys, it is essential to craft questions that are clear, concise, and unbiased. Well-structured questions help to elicit accurate and meaningful responses, avoiding confusion and leading to more reliable data. Incorporating Likert scales, such as a 1-5 rating system, allows for the quantification of responses, making it easier to identify trends and measure the intensity of user opinions. Additionally, segmenting the data according to different user groups, such as demographics or usage patterns, is crucial for uncovering specific needs and preferences within various segments. This segmentation enables a more nuanced analysis, ensuring that insights are tailored to distinct customer groups and helping to inform targeted improvements or strategies.

A **third** measure to **employ is user observations.** Observing users in their natural environment can provide valuable insights into how they interact with a product. This method helps identify usability issues and areas for improvement that may not be captured through interviews or surveys. To gain valuable insights into user interactions, conducting contextual inquiries is essential. This involves observing individuals as they perform tasks related to the offering, helping them to understand their workflow and identify any challenges they face. By closely monitoring how persons engage in their natural environment, you can uncover nuances that might not be apparent through other research methods. It is also important to note behavioral patterns, paying close attention to recurring behaviors or difficulties that users encounter during their interactions. These observations can reveal underlying issues or inefficiencies in the design. To achieve a more comprehensive understanding of personal needs, it is beneficial to combine these observational insights with other research methods, such as surveys or interviews. This multi-method approach provides a more holistic view of user experiences and ensures that the resulting insights are robust and actionable.

Another method is **via analytics and data analysis**. Utilizing data from analytics tools provides a quantitative perspective on how users interact with a product. Metrics such as user engagement, conversion rates, and drop-off points can reveal valuable insights into individual behavior. Tracking key metrics is crucial for understanding user engagement and product performance. Monitoring relevant data points, such as active users, session duration, and feature usage, provides valuable insights into how users interact with the offering. By analyzing this data, you can identify patterns or anomalies that may reveal user preferences or potential issues. For instance, a sudden drop in session duration might indicate a problem with user engagement. To further refine and validate these insights, employing A/B testing is highly effective. A/B tests allow you to compare different versions of features or changes to evaluate their impact on individual behavior and satisfaction. This approach helps ensure that modifications are based on empirical evidence, leading to more informed decisions and enhanced user experiences.

Persona Development is another method employed to understand customer behavior. Personas are fictional representations of ideal users based on research data. Creating detailed personas helps product managers keep user needs and characteristics at the forefront of decision-making. To create effective personas, it's essential to base them on thorough research. This involves gathering data through interviews, surveys, and observations to ensure a deep understanding of the target audience. Detailed profiles should be crafted, incorporating a range of information such as demographics, goals, challenges, and behaviors to provide a comprehensive view of each person. Additionally, it's important to regularly update these personas as new data and insights become available, ensuring they stay accurate and relevant over time.

Customer Journey Mapping is also another method that can be used. Customer journey maps visualize the entire experience a user has with a product, from initial awareness to post-purchase support. This method helps identify touch points, pain points, and opportunities for improvement. To enhance user experience effectively, start by mapping out the key stages of the customer journey, including all interactions with various touch points. This comprehensive mapping allows for a clear visualization of the person's path and helps in identifying specific pain points where users encounter difficulties or dissatisfaction. By highlighting these problematic areas, you can focus on prioritizing improvements that will have the most significant impact on the overall user experience. Utilizing insights from the journey map ensures that changes are made strategically, addressing the most critical issues and enhancing the overall client satisfaction.

Incorporating User Feedback into Product Development

Effectively integrating user feedback into the product development process is crucial for creating products that align with customer needs and expectations. Here's how to ensure that user feedback translates into actionable improvements.

Create a Feedback Loop: Establishing a continuous feedback loop ensures that user insights are consistently gathered, analyzed, and acted upon throughout the product lifecycle. There are several ways to achieve this. Implement mechanisms for ongoing feedback, such as in-app surveys, user forums, or feedback forms. Regularly review feedback to identify common themes, trends, and areas for improvement. Finally, prioritize and implement changes based on user feedback to address identified issues and enhance the product.

Prioritize Feedback: Not all feedback is equally valuable. Prioritizing feedback helps focus efforts on changes that will have the most significant impact on user satisfaction and product success. You can do this by evaluating the impact, considering feasibility and balancing the effects. First, assess the potential impact of each piece of feedback on user experience and business goals. Determine the feasibility of implementing changes based on available resources and technical constraints. Then, balance immediate fixes with long-term improvements to address both urgent issues and strategic goals.

Collaborate with Cross-Functional Teams: Effective product development requires collaboration between various teams, including design, engineering, and marketing. Engaging these teams in the feedback process ensures that user insights are integrated into all aspects of the product. Communicate user feedback and research findings with relevant teams to inform their work. Use feedback to shape product roadmaps and prioritize features or improvements. Ensure to encourage regular discussions and brainstorming sessions with cross-functional teams to address user needs collaboratively.

Iterate and Test: Incorporating user feedback often involves iterative design and development. Testing changes and gathering additional feedback helps refine solutions and ensure they meet user needs. To achieve this, you can go through a process. Create prototypes or beta versions of new features to gather user feedback before full-scale implementation. Test changes with real users to identify any usability issues or areas for improvement. Finally, use feedback from testing to make iterative improvements and refine the product.

Communicate Changes to Users: Transparency with users about how their feedback has influenced product changes can build trust and enhance the user experience. This can be done by sharing updates and acknowledging contributions. Communicate updates and improvements based on user feedback through release notes, newsletters, or in-app notifications. Also, recognize and thank users who provided valuable feedback, reinforcing their engagement and support.

Customer-centric thinking and user research are integral to the role of a product manager. Understanding and prioritizing customer needs through various research methods ensures that products are designed to meet real client demands and solve genuine problems. Incorporating user feedback into the product development process helps create products that are not only functional but also delightful to use. By fostering a culture of continuous learning and improvement, product managers can drive success and create lasting value for both users and the business.

CHAPTER SEVEN

STRATEGIC PLANNING AND SETTING A VISION

Effective strategic planning and vision-setting are cornerstones of successful product management. They not only guide product development but also ensure that the solution aligns with overarching business objectives. This chapter delves into how to create and communicate a compelling product vision and strategy and the critical process of aligning product goals with business objectives.

Creating and Communicating a Product Vision and Strategy

Creating a compelling product vision and developing a coherent strategy are foundational to the success of any product. These elements not only guide the product development process but also ensure that the initiative aligns with the broader business objectives. The process involves crafting a vision statement that encapsulates the product's ultimate goal, formulating a strategic plan to achieve this vision, and effectively communicating both to stakeholders.

The first step is crafting the product vision. This is more than a statement; it is a guiding light that captures the essence of what the product aims to become and the value it seeks to deliver. This vision should be future-oriented, offering a glimpse of the product's impact and ultimate purpose. To craft a vision statement, it is essential to articulate a clear, aspirational goal that resonates with both the team and the target audience. For instance, Spotify's vision is "To unlock the potential of human creativity, by giving a million creative artists the opportunity to live off their art and billions of fans the opportunity to enjoy and be inspired by it." This statement not only describes what Spotify aims to achieve but also highlights the broader impact on artists and fans alike. Similarly, Tesla's vision to "create the most compelling car company of the 21st century by driving the world's transition to electric vehicles" reflects its ambition to lead in innovation and sustainability.

A well-crafted vision statement should be concise and memorable, capable of inspiring and guiding all stakeholders involved in the creation's journey. It should communicate the product's purpose and differentiate it from competitors, providing a sense of direction and motivation.

Next is developing the product strategy. Once the vision is clear, the next step is to develop a strategic plan to achieve it. This involves several critical components, including market analysis, defining the value proposition, setting goals, and creating a roadmap.

Market Analysis is the first step in shaping a strategy. It involves understanding market trends, customer needs, and the competitive landscape. Through customer research, such as surveys and interviews, insights into user needs and pain points can be gathered. Competitive analysis helps identify the strengths and weaknesses of competitors, highlighting opportunities for differentiation. Additionally, trend analysis provides awareness of industry shifts that could influence the product's success. Defining the value proposition is crucial for articulating why customers should choose this product over others. The value proposition should highlight the unique benefits of the product, address specific customer needs, and demonstrate how it stands out from the competition.

Setting Goals and Objectives is **another key** aspect of strategy development. Goals should be **SMART** i.e. Specific, Measurable, Achievable, Relevant, and Time-bound. This ensures that goals are clear and attainable, with metrics in place to track progress and success. Creating a roadmap is essential for visualizing the strategic plan. A product roadmap outlines major phases of development, key milestones, and timelines. It provides a structured approach to achieving strategic goals, helping to coordinate efforts and manage resources effectively.

After a successful conception of an idea, a **major** step is communicating the vision and strategy. Effective communication of both components is vital for alignment and engagement among stakeholders. This involves both internal and external communication.

Internal communication should focus on ensuring that team members understand the vision and strategy and how their work contributes to achieving these goals. Developing a narrative around the vision helps make it relatable and inspiring. Engaging the team through discussions and regular updates fosters a sense of ownership and motivation. Transparency about progress and any changes to the strategy helps maintain alignment and support. External communication involves articulating the vision and strategy to customers, investors, and partners. An elevator pitch can succinctly capture the essence of the vision and strategy, while marketing materials such as brochures and presentations can further elaborate on the product's value proposition and strategic direction. For investors, detailed briefings that outline the vision and strategy can help secure funding and support.

In summary, creating and communicating a product vision and strategy involves crafting an inspiring vision statement, developing a strategic plan that includes market analysis, value proposition, goal setting, and roadmaps, and effectively communicating these elements to both internal and external stakeholders. A well-defined vision and strategy not only guide product development but also ensure that the product aligns with broader business objectives, driving success and achieving long-term goals.

Aligning Product Goals with Business Objectives

Business objectives are broad goals that an organization aims to achieve, such as increasing revenue, expanding market share, or enhancing customer satisfaction. Aligning product goals with these objectives ensures that the solution contributes to the company's overall success. To align these goals, first identify the key business objectives. This may involve:

Consulting Leadership: Engage with executive leaders to understand their strategic priorities.

Reviewing Strategic Plans: Examine company-wide strategic plans and annual reports to identify relevant objectives.

Analyzing Performance Metrics: Assess current performance metrics to identify areas for improvement and alignment.

Once business objectives are clear, align product goals to support them. This involves:

Mapping Objectives to Goals: Ensure that each product goal directly contributes to achieving business objectives. Create a matrix or alignment chart that links each product goal to specific business objectives. This visual representation helps ensure that all product efforts are directed toward supporting overarching company goals.

Setting KPIs: Establish key performance indicators (KPIs) that measure progress toward both product and business goals. KPIs should be relevant, quantifiable and actionable. Relevant means directly related to both product and business goals. Quantifiable refers to measurable in terms of numbers or percentages and actionable means provide insights that can inform decision-making and adjustments.

Prioritizing Initiatives: Focus on product initiatives that will have the greatest impact on achieving business objectives. Evaluate these initiatives based on their potential impact on business objectives. Prioritize those that offer the most significant benefits or address the most critical challenges.

Regularly monitor progress toward both product and business goals. Use KPIs and other performance metrics to track success and identify areas for improvement. Be prepared to adjust strategies and goals based on new data, changing market conditions, or shifts in business priorities. **These are several means to achieve this:**

Regular Reviews: Conduct regular reviews of progress, such as quarterly or bi-annual evaluations. This allows for timely adjustments and ensures ongoing alignment with business objectives.

Adapting to Change: Stay flexible and responsive to changes in the market, technology, or company strategy. Adjust product goals and strategies as needed to maintain alignment with evolving business objectives.

Building a Collaborative Strategy Development Process

Effective strategic planning requires collaboration across various departments and levels within an organization. This section will explore how to build a collaborative process for developing and refining the product vision and strategy.

Collaboration between different teams such as product management, marketing, sales, and customer support is essential for developing a robust product strategy. Each department brings unique insights and expertise that can significantly enrich the strategic planning process. To foster effective cross-functional collaboration, start by establishing cross-functional teams. These teams should include representatives from all relevant departments, each contributing their specialized knowledge to the development of the product vision and strategy.

Regular meetings or workshops are crucial for maintaining alignment and addressing challenges collaboratively. During these sessions, team members can share insights, discuss potential obstacles, and coordinate efforts to ensure that the product strategy reflects a comprehensive understanding of the market and customer needs. Encouraging open communication is also vital. Creating an environment where team members feel comfortable sharing their ideas and feedback helps in uncovering valuable perspectives and building a unified approach to strategy development.

Stakeholder feedback is another critical component of the collaborative process. Engaging with stakeholders such as executives, customers, and partners provides valuable input that can refine and enhance the product vision and strategy. Conducting stakeholder interviews is an effective way to gather diverse perspectives and understand the expectations of key stakeholders. These interviews can reveal critical insights into how the product can better align with business objectives or address market demands.

Surveys and polls are useful tools for collecting quantitative data on stakeholder preferences and priorities. They allow for the aggregation of feedback from a broader audience, offering a clearer picture of stakeholder expectations. Holding feedback sessions where strategic ideas are presented and discussed in real-time can also be beneficial. These sessions facilitate immediate feedback and foster a more interactive and engaging approach to strategy development.

Implementing a structured feedback loop is essential for continuous improvement of the product strategy. Collecting and analyzing this information regularly helps identify trends and areas for adjustment. Feedback should be systematically gathered from all relevant parties and reviewed to extract actionable insights. Integrating this feedback into the strategy ensures that the product evolves in response to stakeholder input and market changes.

Effective communication of any changes or updates to the strategy is crucial for maintaining alignment and support. By clearly conveying how feedback has influenced strategic decisions, you reinforce the value of stakeholder input and keep all parties informed and engaged in the process.

Incorporating data and analytics into planning is increasingly critical for making informed decisions and guiding product development. Data-driven insights enhance the accuracy of forecasts, improve understanding of market dynamics, and ensure that strategies are based on empirical evidence rather than intuition alone.

Market research is foundational to informed strategic planning. It involves gathering and analyzing data on market conditions, customer behavior, and competitive dynamics. Quantitative research methods, such as surveys and data analytics, provide numerical insights into market trends and customer preferences. These methods offer measurable and objective data that can guide strategic decisions.

Qualitative research, including interviews and focus groups, provides deeper insights into customer needs and motivations. By understanding the underlying reasons behind customer behaviors and preferences, you can tailor your product strategy to better address these factors.

Monitoring and analyzing the performance is crucial for assessing the effectiveness of your strategy. Performance metrics, such as user engagement, conversion rates, and revenue growth, offer insights into how well the product is meeting its goals. User analytics tools, like Google Analytics or Mix panel, allow for the tracking of user behavior and identification of patterns or issues that may require attention. A/B testing is another valuable technique for evaluating different versions of features or strategies. By comparing the performance of various options, you can determine which approach is more effective and make data-informed decisions.

Predictive analytics plays a vital role in forecasting future trends and informing tactical decisions. By analyzing historical data, you can identify patterns and anticipate future market trends. Customer segmentation, based on data analysis, allows for more targeted strategies tailored to different segments' needs and behaviors. Scenario planning, using predictive models, helps anticipate potential changes and prepare strategic responses.

To ensure that data informs proper planning, base decisions on empirical evidence rather than intuition. Data-driven decision-making involves using quantitative and qualitative data to guide strategic choices. Data visualization tools, such as dashboards, help present complex data in an accessible and actionable format. Regular review of data sources and analytics methods ensures that they remain relevant and effective, enabling continuous refinement of the strategy based on the latest insights.

Strategic planning and vision-setting are critical for guiding product development and ensuring alignment with business objectives. By crafting a clear and compelling product vision, developing a strategic plan, and effectively communicating these elements, you can create a strong foundation for success. Aligning product goals with business objectives ensures that your solution contributes to the overall success of the organization, driving growth and achieving strategic priorities. Regular monitoring and adjustment of strategies and goals will help you stay on course and adapt to changing circumstances, ensuring long-term success and relevance in the market.

CHAPTER EIGHT

MANAGING PRODUCT ROADMAPS AND PRIORITIZATION

Product roadmaps are crucial tools for guiding the development and evolution of a product. They outline the vision, strategy, and tactical plans, serving as a blueprint for these development teams. Effective roadmap management and prioritization ensure that resources are allocated efficiently, short-term needs are met, and long-term goals are achieved. This chapter delves into techniques for creating and maintaining roadmaps, balancing immediate requirements with strategic objectives, and integrating stakeholder input into the process.

Techniques for Roadmap Creation and Maintenance

Creating and maintaining a product roadmap involves a series of steps and best practices designed to ensure that it remains a valuable and actionable tool throughout the product lifecycle. These are the steps to take.

Define Objectives and Goals: The first step in roadmap creation is to define the product's objectives and goals. These should be aligned with the overall product vision and business strategy. Objectives should be clear, measurable, and achievable, providing a foundation for the roadmap. They should articulate what the product aims to achieve and include specific, measurable targets. For example, increasing user engagement by 20% or launching a new feature by a certain date. Ensure that the roadmap objectives support broader business goals, such as market expansion, revenue growth, or customer satisfaction.

Identify Key Initiatives: Once objectives are set, identify key initiatives that will drive progress towards these goals. Initiatives are high-level efforts or projects that will help achieve the roadmap objectives. Gather input from various teams, including product management, engineering, marketing, and customer support, to generate a list of potential initiatives. Evaluate initiatives based on their impact, feasibility, and alignment with objectives. Prioritization should consider factors such as market demand, customer needs, and resource availability.

Develop a Roadmap Framework: The roadmap framework is the structure that organizes and visualizes initiatives, timelines, and milestones. Common frameworks include timeline, goal oriented and feature based. Timeline based roadmap displays initiatives along a timeline, showing when each will be worked on and completed. Goal-oriented focuses on achieving specific goals or outcomes, with initiatives grouped by the objectives they support. Feature-based highlights planned features and enhancements, detailing their development and release schedule.

Create and Maintain the Roadmap: With the framework in place, develop the roadmap by detailing the initiatives, timelines, and resources required. Regular maintenance is crucial to keep the roadmap up-to-date and relevant. For each initiative, include details such as objectives, timelines, milestones, dependencies, and responsible teams. Schedule regular reviews and updates to reflect changes in priorities, new insights, or shifts in the market. Maintain flexibility to adapt to evolving needs and conditions.

Communicate the Roadmap: Effective communication of the roadmap is essential for ensuring alignment and transparency. Internal communication is to share the roadmap with internal teams to ensure everyone understands the objectives, initiatives, and timelines. Regularly update teams on progress and changes. External communication involves communicating key aspects of the roadmap to stakeholders, such as customers and partners, to manage expectations and gather feedback.

Balancing Short-Term Needs with Long-Term Goals

Managing product roadmaps involves striking a balance between addressing immediate needs and achieving long-term strategic goals. This balance is critical for maintaining product relevance and ensuring sustained success.

Short-term needs often arise from pressing customer demands, evolving market conditions, or operational challenges. These immediate concerns can significantly impact user satisfaction and competitive positioning. Identifying and responding to these short-term needs is crucial, as it allows for quick wins that can enhance the product's appeal and relevance in the market. For instance, urgent bug fixes or feature requests from key customers must be prioritized to prevent dissatisfaction and maintain customer loyalty. Evaluating the impact of addressing these short-term needs involves considering their benefits relative to overall product goals and available resources. Prioritization techniques, such as the Eisenhower Matrix or MoSCoW Method, can help in making these decisions by weighing the urgency and impact of each task.

On the other hand, long-term goals guide the overarching direction and strategic development of the product. These goals should align with the broader product vision and business strategy, focusing on achieving substantial milestones such as entering new markets, advancing technological capabilities, or establishing significant competitive advantages. Defining clear and strategic long-term goals provides a roadmap for sustained growth and innovation. It is essential that these goals are well-integrated into the roadmap, with defined initiatives and milestones that support their achievement.

Balancing short-term and long-term priorities requires a strategic approach to resource allocation and prioritization. Effective prioritization involves assessing how immediate needs align with or potentially impact long-term objectives. While it is important to address urgent issues, it should not come at the expense of long-term goals. Allocating resources judiciously means supporting immediate needs without undermining the progress of long-term initiatives. This may involve adjusting timelines or reallocating resources based on the relative importance of short-term versus long-term goals.

Regularly reviewing and adjusting the roadmap is critical to maintaining this balance. Periodic reviews of the roadmap help assess progress, realign priorities, and make necessary adjustments based on new insights or shifting market conditions. Soliciting feedback from internal teams, customers, and stakeholders can provide valuable input for these adjustments, ensuring that the roadmap remains relevant and responsive to both immediate and strategic needs. By managing this balance effectively, organizations can achieve a harmonious integration of short-term successes with the pursuit of long-term vision, driving sustained product success and growth.

Incorporating stakeholder input is essential for developing a product roadmap that effectively addresses diverse needs and expectations. Engaging with stakeholders, including customers, partners, and internal teams ensures that the roadmap is comprehensive and aligns with the broader goals of those invested in the product's success.

Gathering insights from these individuals involves using various methods to capture their perspectives. Surveys and interviews are valuable tools for obtaining direct feedback, revealing critical pain points, desired features, and areas for improvement. Analyzing this feedback allows organizations to identify common themes and priorities, which can be integrated into the roadmap. Additionally, conducting collaborative workshops or brainstorming sessions offers an interactive platform for stakeholders to contribute ideas and refine initiatives. This inclusive approach helps ensure that the roadmap reflects a wide range of viewpoints and needs.

Transparent communication is key to managing expectations and ensuring that their input is effectively incorporated. Clearly articulating how feedback has been used to shape the product strategy and roadmap helps maintain transparency and build trust. Regular updates on progress, changes, and challenges keep stakeholders informed and engaged, reinforcing the value of their contributions. Setting clear expectations regarding timelines, deliverables, and potential trade-offs is also important. By outlining what stakeholders can anticipate from the product development process, organizations align expectations with the practical realities of development. Ongoing communication about the status of their input and the overall direction of the product ensures continued engagement and support.

Managing product roadmaps and prioritization is a multifaceted process that involves creating a structured roadmap, balancing short-term and long-term objectives, and incorporating stakeholder input. By employing effective techniques for roadmap creation and maintenance, balancing immediate needs with strategic goals, and engaging stakeholders throughout the process, organizations can develop and execute a strategy that drives success and achieves both short-term wins and long-term objectives. Regular reviews and adjustments ensure that the roadmap remains relevant and effective, guiding the product through its lifecycle and positioning it for sustained success.

CHAPTER NINE

NAVIGATING CHALLENGES AND MAKING TOUGH DECISIONS

Product management is an intricate field, often fraught with various challenges. Navigating these challenges effectively is crucial for steering a product toward success. This section outlines twelve common challenges faced by product managers and offers strategies to overcome them. Understanding these challenges and their corresponding strategies can significantly enhance a product manager's ability to lead teams, drive product development, and deliver value.

Common Challenges Faced by Product Managers and Strategies to Overcome Them

Balancing Short-Term and Long-Term Priorities: One of the primary challenges product managers faces is balancing short-term needs with long-term strategic goals. Short-term demands, such as urgent bug fixes or immediate feature requests, can often overshadow long-term objectives. Implement a prioritization framework to balance these demands effectively.

Techniques like the Eisenhower Matrix or MoSCoW Method can help categorize tasks by urgency and importance. Regularly review and adjust the roadmap to ensure alignment with both immediate needs and strategic goals. Additionally, setting clear milestones for long-term objectives can help maintain focus and progress.

Managing Stakeholder Expectations: Product managers frequently contend with varied expectations from stakeholders, including executives, customers, and team members. Aligning these expectations with what is feasible and realistic can be challenging. Establish clear and open lines of communication with stakeholders. Regularly update them on progress, changes, and any trade-offs that may be necessary. Use their feedback to inform decision-making and manage expectations through transparent reporting and well-defined project goals.

Navigating Conflicting Priorities: Conflicting priorities among different teams or departments can create obstacles in full cycle development. For instance, engineering might prioritize technical stability, while marketing may push for faster feature releases. Foster cross-functional collaboration through regular alignment meetings and workshops. Develop a shared understanding of objectives and constraints and use prioritization techniques to reconcile conflicting priorities. Ensure that all teams are aligned with the product vision and strategic goals to facilitate smoother decision-making.

Adapting to Changing Market Conditions: The market landscape can shift rapidly due to technological advancements, competitor actions, or changing customer preferences. Adapting to these changes while maintaining product direction can be difficult. Implement agile methodologies to respond quickly to market changes. Conduct regular market research and competitive analysis to stay informed about trends and emerging opportunities. Maintain flexibility in the product roadmap to accommodate necessary adjustments based on market dynamics.

Ensuring Effective Communication: Effective communication is vital for product managers to coordinate with team members, stakeholders, and customers. Miscommunication or lack of clarity can lead to project delays and misunderstandings. Establish clear communication channels and protocols. Utilize tools such as project management software, regular team meetings, and status reports to keep everyone informed. Ensure that all stakeholders receive consistent and accurate updates to minimize misunderstandings.

Prioritizing Features and Enhancements: Deciding which features or enhancements to prioritize can be challenging, especially when there are competing demands from different stakeholders or customers. Use data-driven approaches to prioritize features based on factors such as customer impact, business value, and feasibility. Techniques like the Value vs. Effort Matrix can help evaluate and rank features. Engage with customers to understand their needs and use this feedback to guide prioritization decisions.

Managing Resources and Budget Constraints: Product managers often face constraints related to resources and budget, which can impact the scope and timeline of product development. Develop a detailed project plan and budget that outlines resource requirements and costs. Prioritize initiatives based on available resources and adjust the scope or timeline as needed. Regularly review resource allocation and budget adherence to ensure alignment with project goals.

Handling Team Dynamics and Conflicts: Team dynamics and conflicts can affect productivity and morale. Addressing interpersonal issues or differing opinions requires skillful management. Foster a positive team culture through open communication, team-building activities, and conflict resolution strategies. Encourage collaboration and provide opportunities for team members to voice their concerns and ideas. Address conflicts promptly and constructively to maintain a cohesive and productive team environment.

Managing Risk and Uncertainty: Product development involves inherent risks and uncertainties, such as technological challenges, market risks, or unforeseen obstacles. Conduct thorough risk assessments to identify potential risks and develop mitigation strategies. Use risk management techniques, such as creating contingency plans and performing regular risk reviews, to address uncertainties. Maintain a proactive approach to identify and address potential issues before they escalate.

Maintaining Customer Focus: Keeping the product aligned with customer needs and preferences can be challenging, particularly when balancing these needs with technical constraints or business goals. Engage with customers regularly through surveys, interviews, and user testing to gather feedback and understand their needs. Incorporate customer insights into the product development process and use this feedback to guide decision-making. Ensure that the product roadmap reflects customer priorities and addresses their pain points.

Aligning with Company Vision and Strategy: Ensuring that the creation aligns with the overall company vision and strategic objectives can be challenging, especially in rapidly changing environments. Develop a clear understanding of the company's vision and strategic goals. Consistently review and align the product roadmap with these objectives. Communicate the product vision and strategy to all team members and stakeholders to ensure that everyone is working towards common goals.

Managing Time and Workload: Product managers often juggle multiple responsibilities, including strategic planning, team management, and stakeholder communication. Managing time and workload effectively is crucial for maintaining productivity and focus. Prioritize tasks based on their importance and impact. Use time management techniques, such as the Pomodoro Technique or time blocking, to stay focused and organized. Delegate tasks where possible and ensure that you have a well-structured schedule to manage competing demands efficiently.

Professionals in this field face a range of challenges that require effective strategies and proactive management. By balancing short-term and long-term priorities, managing stakeholder expectations, navigating conflicting priorities, and addressing other common issues, product managers can lead their teams to success and drive product development effectively. Adopting these strategies helps ensure that products are developed in alignment with both immediate needs and strategic goals, ultimately contributing to the overall success of the product and the organization.

Decision-Making Frameworks and Tools

Effective decision-making is at the heart of successful full cycle development and the track record of a professional. Product managers frequently face complex decisions that require a structured approach to ensure the best outcomes. Decision-making frameworks and tools provide systematic methods for evaluating options, analyzing data, and reaching well-informed conclusions. We will examine several key decision-making frameworks and tools that can aid product managers in navigating the complexities of their roles.

One foundational tool for decision-making is the Eisenhower Matrix, also known as the Urgent-Important Matrix. This framework helps prioritize tasks based on their urgency and importance. The matrix divides tasks into four quadrants: Urgent and Important, Not Urgent but Important, Urgent but Not Important, and Not Urgent and Not Important. Tasks categorized as Urgent and Important should be addressed immediately, while those that are Not Urgent but Important should be scheduled for future attention. Urgent but Not Important tasks are often candidates for delegation, and those Not Urgent and Not Important can be deferred or eliminated. Using the Eisenhower Matrix helps product managers allocate their time and resources efficiently, focusing on what truly matters and preventing less critical tasks from consuming valuable attention.

Another valuable framework is the MoSCoW Method, which is used for prioritizing features, requirements, or tasks. This method categorizes items into four groups: Must Have, Should Have, Could Have, and Won't Have (This Time). Must Have items are essential for the project's success and should be prioritized above all else. Should Have items are important but not critical and Could Have items are desirable but not necessary. Finally, Won't Have (This Time) items are excluded from the current scope but might be revisited later. By applying this method, product experts can effectively manage scope and ensure that the most crucial elements are addressed first.

The RICE Scoring Model offers another structured approach for prioritizing initiatives. RICE stands for Reach, Impact, Confidence, and Effort. Reach refers to the number of people affected by the feature or change, Impact measures the potential effect or benefit, Confidence assesses the certainty about estimates and assumptions, and Effort evaluates the resources required for implementation. By scoring each option based on these criteria, product managers can make data-driven decisions and balance various factors to prioritize effectively.

The Value vs. Effort Matrix is a practical tool for evaluating tasks or features based on their potential value and the effort required to implement them. This matrix divides tasks into four categories: High Value, Low Effort; High Value, High Effort; Low Value, Low Effort; and Low Value, High Effort. High Value, Low Effort tasks are typically prioritized for quick wins, while High Value, High Effort tasks, though demanding, are important for strategic goals. Low Value, Low Effort tasks can be addressed as minor improvements, while Low Value, High Effort tasks are often deprioritized unless absolutely necessary. This matrix helps teams focus on initiatives that deliver the greatest return on investment with the least amount of effort.

SWOT Analysis is a strategic planning tool used to identify Strengths, Weaknesses, Opportunities, and Threats related to a product or project. Strengths are internal attributes that offer advantages, Weaknesses are internal challenges, Opportunities are external factors that could be leveraged for growth, and Threats are external risks that could impact success. By conducting a SWOT Analysis, product managers can gain a comprehensive understanding of the strategic landscape, identify key areas for improvement, and develop strategies to capitalize on opportunities while mitigating threats.

The Decision Matrix, or Prioritization Matrix, helps product experts evaluate and compare multiple options based on predefined criteria. This tool involves defining criteria, scoring each option against these criteria, and assigning weights based on their importance. By calculating weighted scores, product managers can objectively compare options and prioritize based on a structured evaluation of relevant factors. This approach ensures that decisions are made based on a thorough analysis rather than intuition alone.

The Delphi Method is a structured process for obtaining expert opinions through iterative rounds of surveys or questionnaires. Experts provide initial responses, which are aggregated and shared with the group. Subsequent rounds allow experts to revise their responses based on feedback from others. This iterative process helps build consensus and refine estimates or opinions. The Delphi Method is particularly useful for addressing complex or uncertain issues where expert insights can provide valuable guidance.

Cost-Benefit Analysis involves comparing the costs and benefits of different options to determine the most advantageous course of action. This analysis requires identifying all costs associated with each option, estimating the expected benefits, and calculating the net benefits by subtracting costs from benefits. By conducting a Cost-Benefit Analysis, product managers can evaluate the financial implications of various decisions and prioritize options that offer the highest net benefits.

The Impact/Effort Matrix is similar to the Value vs. Effort Matrix but focuses specifically on evaluating the impact and effort involved in implementing a solution. This matrix categorizes tasks or initiatives into High Impact, Low Effort; High Impact, High Effort; Low Impact, Low Effort; and Low Impact, High Effort. Prioritizing High Impact, Low Effort solutions ensures that valuable initiatives are implemented efficiently, while High Impact High Effort initiatives are considered for strategic planning.

Scenario Planning involves developing and analyzing different scenarios to anticipate future uncertainties and their potential impact on decisions. This method requires identifying key uncertainties, creating various scenarios based on these uncertainties, and evaluating the implications of each scenario. Scenario Planning helps product managers prepare for potential future conditions, making their decisions more robust and adaptable to changing circumstances.

The Pareto Principle, also known as the 80/20 Rule, posits that approximately 80% of effects come from 20% of causes. This principle helps identify the most significant factors contributing to results, allowing product managers to focus their efforts on high-impact areas. By addressing the key causes that generate the majority of results, product managers can optimize their strategies and achieve more efficient outcomes.

Finally, User Story Mapping is a technique for visualizing the user journey and organizing user stories or tasks based on their importance and sequence. This approach involves mapping out user interactions and breaking them down into manageable tasks, which are then prioritized according to their relevance to the user journey and business goals. User Story Mapping provides a structured approach to prioritizing and managing tasks, ensuring that product development aligns with user needs and delivers value.

Case Studies and Real-World Applications

This section on case studies and real-world applications provides practical insights into how decision-making frameworks and tools can be effectively used. This section will help you understand the practical implementation of these strategies, learn from real-world examples, and apply best practices in their own product management roles. It adds depth by linking theoretical concepts with practical experiences, making the content more relatable and actionable for product managers.

Introduction to Case Studies

Explain the importance of case studies in understanding the practical application of decision-making frameworks.

Discuss how real-world examples can offer valuable insights and lessons for product managers.

Implementing the Eisenhower Matrix

Background: Describe the context and challenges faced by the company or product team.

Application: Explain how the Eisenhower Matrix was used to prioritize tasks and manage project workflows.

Outcome: Discuss the results and how prioritization impacted project success and team productivity.

Using the MoSCoW Method for Feature Prioritization

Background: Outline the project or product development scenario where the MoSCoW Method was applied.

Application: Detail the process of categorizing features and managing stakeholder expectations.

Outcome: Evaluate the effectiveness of the prioritization and its influence on product delivery and customer satisfaction.

RICE Scoring Model in Product Roadmap Planning

Background: Provide context for the product roadmap planning and the need for prioritization.

Application: Describe how the RICE Scoring Model was used to assess and rank features or initiatives.

Outcome: Highlight the impact on decision-making, resource allocation, and overall project success.

Addressing Conflicting Priorities with the Value vs. Effort Matrix

Background: Identify the conflict or challenge related to prioritizing tasks or features.

Application: Explain how the Value vs. Effort Matrix helped resolve conflicting priorities.

Outcome: Share the results and how the matrix facilitated better decision-making and resource management.

SWOT Analysis for Strategic Planning

Background: Describe a scenario where SWOT Analysis was used for strategic planning.

Application: Detail how strengths, weaknesses, opportunities, and threats were identified and analyzed.

Outcome: Discuss the strategic decisions made based on the SWOT Analysis and their impact on the product or company.

Lessons Learned and Best Practices

Summarize key lessons learned from the case studies.

Highlight best practices for applying decision-making frameworks and tools in real-world situations.

Conclusion

Reflect on the value of case studies in understanding and implementing decision-making strategies.

Emphasize the importance of adapting frameworks and tools to fit specific contexts and challenges.

Navigating the challenges of product management means getting a solid grip on decision-making tools and frameworks. Using structured methods like the Eisenhower Matrix, MoSCoW Method, and RICE Scoring Model helps product managers prioritize tasks, handle competing demands, and make smart choices. Real-world case studies add another layer of insight by showing how these strategies play out in practice, providing real examples and practical tips. Mastering these decision-making tools lets product experts lead their teams effectively, stay aligned with strategic goals, and drive their products to success with confidence.

CHAPTER TEN

METRICS, DATA AND PERFORMANCE EVALUATION

To make progress on this stage, understanding and leveraging metrics, data, and performance evaluation is crucial for driving product success. Metrics and Key Performance Indicators (KPIs) provide the quantitative backbone for assessing a product's health, guiding strategic decisions, and measuring the effectiveness of product initiatives. This chapter delves into essential KPIs for product success and explores how to use data to drive decisions and measure outcomes.

Key Performance Indicators (KPIs) for Product Success

Key Performance Indicators (KPIs) are vital metrics used to gauge the performance and success of a product. They offer measurable values that reflect the product's progress towards its goals and objectives. Selecting the right KPIs is crucial for effective performance management, as they help track success, identify areas for improvement, and align efforts with strategic goals.

Product Adoption Rate: The Product Adoption Rate measures how quickly users are starting to use a new product or feature. It is a critical **indicator of initial market acceptance and can be calculated by:**

{Product Adoption Rate} = {Number of New Users} divided by {Total Target Market} X 100

A high adoption rate suggests that the product or feature is meeting user needs and gaining traction, while a low rate may indicate issues with the product's appeal or market fit.

Customer Retention Rate: Customer Retention Rate measures the percentage of customers who continue to use a product over a specified period. It is an essential KPI for understanding long-term user engagement and loyalty. It is calculated by:

{Customer Retention Rate} = {Number of Customers at End of Period - Number of New Customers} divided by {Number of Customers at Start of Period}} X 100

High retention rates often correlate with strong product value and customer satisfaction, while low rates may highlight issues such as product dissatisfaction or increased competition.

Net Promoter Score (NPS): The Net Promoter Score (NPS) gauges customer satisfaction and loyalty by asking users how likely they are to recommend the product to others. Responses are categorized into Promoters, Passives, and Detractors. It is calculated by:

{NPS} = {Percentage of Promoters - Percentage of Detractors}

A high NPS indicates that customers are enthusiastic about the product and likely to spread positive word-of-mouth, which is crucial for organic growth.

Customer Lifetime Value (CLV): Customer Lifetime Value (CLV) estimates the total revenue a business can expect from a customer over the entire duration of their relationship. It is a valuable metric for assessing the long-term value of customer acquisition and retention efforts. It is calculated by:

{CLV} = {Average Purchase Value} X {Average Purchase Frequency} X {Customer Lifespan}

By understanding CLV, product managers can better allocate resources to customer acquisition and retention strategies.

Churn Rate: Churn Rate measures the percentage of customers who stop using a product within a given period. It is the inverse of retention and is crucial for understanding user attrition. It is calculated by:

{Churn Rate} = {Number of Lost Customers} divided by {Total Number of Customers at Start of Period} X 100

A high churn rate can signal problems with product satisfaction or competitive pressures and may prompt a need for improvements in product features or customer support.

Conversion Rate: Conversion Rate tracks the percentage of users who complete a desired action, such as making a purchase, signing up for a trial, or completing a form. It is calculated by

{Conversion Rate} = {Number of Conversions} divided by {Total Number of Visitors} X 100

High conversion rates indicate that users are engaging effectively with the product's calls-to-action, while low rates may suggest issues with the user experience or marketing effectiveness.

Average Revenue Per User (ARPU): Average Revenue Per User (ARPU) measures the average revenue generated from each user over a specific period. It helps evaluate the revenue potential and performance of the product. It is calculated by:

{ARPU} = {Total Revenue} divided by {Number of Users}

ARPU is valuable for understanding revenue generation efficiency and can guide pricing and monetization strategies.

Product Usage Metrics: Product Usage Metrics include various indicators of how frequently and in what ways users engage with the product. These may include Daily Active Users (DAU) which are the number of unique users engaging with the product daily and Monthly Active Users (MAU) which represent the number of unique users engaging with the product monthly. Tracking DAU and MAU helps assess user engagement and the product's stickiness.

Feature Usage Rate: Feature Usage Rate measures how often specific features of the product are used compared to others. This can reveal which features are most valuable and which may need enhancement. It is calculated by:

{Feature Usage Rate} = {Number of Users Using Feature} divided by {Total Number of Users} X 100

Understanding feature usage helps prioritize development efforts and focus on features that drive user satisfaction.

Customer Satisfaction Score (CSAT): Customer Satisfaction Score (CSAT) is obtained by asking users to rate their satisfaction with the product or service on a scale, typically from 1 to 5. The average score provides insight into overall user satisfaction. It is calculated by:

{CSAT} = {Sum of All Satisfaction Scores} divided by {Number of Responses}

High CSAT scores indicate a positive user experience, while low scores may highlight areas needing improvement.

Cost Per Acquisition (CPA): Cost Per Acquisition (CPA) measures the average cost of acquiring a new customer, including marketing and sales expenses. It is calculated by:

{CPA} = {Total Cost of Acquisition} divided by {Number of New Customers}

CPA helps evaluate the efficiency of marketing and sales efforts and informs budget allocation.

Return on Investment (ROI): Return on Investment (ROI) calculates the profitability of an investment by comparing the gains or losses from the investment to its cost. It is calculated by:

{ROI} = {Net Profit} divided by {Cost of Investment} X 100

ROI provides a measure of the financial return generated by investments in product development, marketing, or other initiatives.

Using Data to Drive Decisions and Measure Outcomes

Once KPIs are established, the next step is using data to drive decisions and measure outcomes. Data-driven decision-making ensures that choices are based on objective evidence rather than intuition alone. Here's how to effectively leverage data in product management.

Effective decision-making starts with robust data collection and integration. This involves gathering data from various sources, such as user interactions, sales transactions, customer feedback, and market research. Integrating data from different sources into a centralized system, such as a Customer Data Platform (CDP) or Business Intelligence (BI) tool, ensures that all relevant information is accessible and actionable. Analyzing data trends involves examining historical data to identify patterns and trends over time. This can include tracking changes in KPIs, user behavior, and market conditions. Techniques such as trend analysis, regression analysis, and cohort analysis can provide insights into how different factors impact product performance and user engagement.

A/B testing, or split testing, is a method of comparing two versions of a product or feature to determine which performs better. By randomly assigning users to different versions and measuring their responses, product managers can make data-driven decisions about which changes to implement. This approach helps optimize product features and user experiences based on real user feedback.

User segmentation involves dividing users into distinct groups based on characteristics such as demographics, behavior, or preferences. By analyzing data from different user segments, product managers can tailor features, messaging, and marketing efforts to meet the specific needs of each group. This targeted approach enhances user engagement and improves product effectiveness. Regularly monitoring performance metrics is essential for tracking progress towards goals and identifying areas for improvement. Product managers should establish a routine for reviewing KPIs and other relevant metrics, using dashboards and reporting tools to visualize data and gain actionable insights. This ongoing monitoring helps ensure that the product remains aligned with strategic objectives and can adapt to changing conditions.

Predictive analytics uses historical data and statistical models to forecast future outcomes and trends. By applying predictive models, product managers can anticipate user behavior, market changes, and potential challenges. This proactive approach enables better planning and decision-making, allowing teams to address issues before they become significant problems.

Data-driven decision-making involves using insights from data analysis to guide strategic choices and actions. Product managers should prioritize decisions based on evidence rather than assumptions, using data to validate hypotheses and evaluate potential outcomes. This approach reduces uncertainty and increases the likelihood of successful product initiatives. Measuring and evaluating outcomes involves assessing the results of product changes, initiatives, or strategies against established KPIs. This evaluation process helps determine whether goals have been met, whether the desired impact has been achieved, and what adjustments may be needed. Regularly reviewing outcomes ensures that the product continues to meet user needs and aligns with business objectives.

Iterative development based on user feedback is a key aspect of data-driven product management. Collecting and analyzing feedback from users, both quantitative (e.g., surveys, usage data) and qualitative (e.g., interviews, focus groups), provides valuable insights into product performance and areas for improvement. Product managers should use this feedback to make iterative changes and enhancements, ensuring that the product evolves to better meet user expectations.

While quantitative data (e.g., KPIs, usage metrics) provides objective measures of performance, qualitative data (e.g., user feedback, reviews) offers contextual insights into user experiences and preferences. Balancing both types of data allows product managers to gain a comprehensive understanding of product performance and make well-rounded decisions. Communicating insights effectively involves presenting data and findings in a clear and actionable manner. Product managers should use visualizations, such as charts and graphs, to convey key metrics and trends. Providing context and explanations helps stakeholders understand the significance of the data and supports informed decision-making.

Building a data-driven culture within the organization involves promoting the importance of data and analytics in decision-making processes. Encouraging team members to embrace data-driven approaches, providing training on data analysis tools, and fostering a culture of curiosity and evidence-based thinking contribute to better decision-making and improved solution outcomes.

Advanced Data Analytics Techniques for Product Management

This section explores sophisticated data analytics methods that go beyond basic KPI tracking and offer deeper insights into product performance and user behavior. Advanced analytics techniques can reveal patterns, predict future trends, and provide actionable intelligence for strategic decision-making.

Predictive Analytics: Predictive analytics involves using statistical models and machine learning algorithms to forecast future events based on historical data. For product managers, predictive analytics can be applied to various aspects, such as predicting how users might interact with new features or respond to changes in the product. It can also be helpful in identifying which users are likely to stop using the product and developing strategies to retain them. Finally, it is used in estimating future product demand based on trends and market conditions.

Cohort Analysis: Cohort analysis is a method of examining data by grouping users based on shared characteristics or behaviors over time. This technique helps in comparing the retention of different user cohorts to understand how different groups engage with the product. It is also used in analyzing how usage patterns evolve among different cohorts, which can inform feature development and marketing strategies.

Sentiment Analysis: This analysis uses natural language processing (NLP) to analyze user feedback and reviews, extracting sentiment and emotional tone. It helps in gauging overall user satisfaction and sentiment towards the product or specific features and detecting recurring themes or issues mentioned by users to address them proactively.

Machine Learning and AI: Machine learning (ML) and artificial intelligence (AI) can enhance product management by using algorithms to recommend features or content based on individual user behavior and preferences. It is also used in automating the analysis of large datasets to uncover hidden patterns and trends that may not be immediately apparent.

Data Visualization Techniques: Effective data visualization techniques help in presenting complex data in an understandable manner. This includes using tools like Tableau or Power BI to create interactive dashboards that allow for real-time data exploration and visualizing data geographically to identify regional trends or issues.

A/B Testing with Statistical Rigor: A/B testing is not just about comparing two versions but doing so with statistical rigor. This includes sample size calculation which is ensuring that the sample size is adequate to detect meaningful differences between variants. It is also understanding and applying statistical significance to ensure that results are not due to chance.

Building and Maintaining a Data-Driven Culture

Creating and sustaining a data-driven culture within an organization is crucial for maximizing the benefits of metrics and data. This section focuses on the strategies and practices required to foster a culture where data-driven decision-making is the norm. Key points include:

Establishing a Data-Driven Vision: Setting a clear vision for a data-driven approach requires securing leadership buy-in and ensuring strategic alignment. First and foremost, gaining support from senior leadership is crucial. When top executives champion data-driven practices, it signals their commitment to prioritizing these methods across the organization. This endorsement helps in allocating necessary resources and fostering an environment where data-driven decision-making is encouraged and valued. Additionally, aligning data initiatives with the organization's overall strategic goals is essential. By ensuring that data efforts are directly linked to broader business objectives, organizations can guarantee that data initiatives contribute meaningfully to their long-term success. This strategic alignment helps in creating a cohesive approach where data is used not just for its own sake but as a tool to drive key business outcomes and fulfill organizational ambitions.

Implementing Data Literacy Programs: Enhancing data literacy among team members is crucial for effective data utilization within an organization. To achieve this, implementing comprehensive training programs is essential. These programs should focus on equipping team members with the skills needed to use data analysis tools, techniques, and interpretation methods effectively. By providing targeted training, organizations ensure that all employees are capable of analyzing and leveraging data to support their roles and decision-making processes. Additionally, conducting workshops and seminars plays a key role in deepening understanding of data-driven decision-making and best practices. These interactive sessions offer opportunities for team members to engage with data in practical settings, share insights, and learn from experts. Such initiatives foster a culture where data literacy is prioritized, ultimately enhancing the organization's overall ability to make informed, and data-driven decisions.

Integrating Data Across Teams: Ensuring that data flows seamlessly across different teams and departments involves utilizing data integration tools and fostering cross-functional collaboration. Employing data integration tools is crucial for consolidating information from various sources into a centralized repository. This approach ensures that data is consistent, accessible, and up to date across the organization. Concurrently, encouraging collaboration between teams such as product, marketing, sales, and customer support is essential for sharing insights and data effectively. By promoting open communication and collaboration, organizations can leverage diverse perspectives and expertise, leading to more informed decision-making and a unified approach to data management. This seamless flow of data and collaboration enhances overall efficiency and ensures that all departments work with the most accurate and comprehensive information available.

Creating a Data Governance Framework: A robust data governance framework is essential for ensuring data quality, security, and compliance. Establishing data quality standards is a fundamental component, as it involves implementing rigorous practices to maintain accuracy and consistency in data. These standards ensure that data remains reliable and trustworthy, which is crucial for making informed decisions. Equally important is addressing data privacy and security. Ensuring compliance with data privacy regulations helps protect sensitive information from unauthorized access or breaches, safeguarding both the organization and its customers. By focusing on these aspects, a strong data governance framework not only upholds the integrity and confidentiality of data but also supports overall organizational accountability and trust.

Encouraging Data-Driven Innovation: Promoting a culture of innovation based on data involves fostering an environment where experimentation and recognition of successes are integral to the organization's practices. Encouraging teams to experiment with data-driven approaches allows them to explore new methods, test hypotheses, and learn from the results. This iterative process not only drives innovation but also helps refine strategies and improve decision-making. Additionally, recognizing and celebrating successes plays a crucial role in reinforcing the value of data-driven decisions. By sharing stories of how data-driven approaches have led to positive outcomes, organizations can inspire others and validate the effectiveness of their data initiatives. This recognition not only motivates teams but also helps embed a culture where data-driven innovation is actively pursued and valued.

Measuring and Evaluating the Impact of Data Initiatives: Assessing the effectiveness of data-driven initiatives involves conducting a thorough impact assessment and establishing feedback loops. Impact assessment requires measuring how data initiatives affect business outcomes, such as improvements in efficiency or increases in revenue. This evaluation helps determine whether the data strategies are meeting their objectives and contributing to the organization's goals. Equally important is the creation of feedback loops, which are essential for continuously refining data practices. By gathering feedback on the performance and challenges of data initiatives, organizations can make informed adjustments and improvements. This iterative process ensures that data practices remain relevant and effective, helping to address any issues promptly and adapt to evolving needs. Together, impact assessment and feedback loops provide a comprehensive approach to evaluating and enhancing the effectiveness of data-driven initiatives.

Metrics, data, and performance evaluation are fundamental to successful product management. By focusing on key performance indicators and leveraging data-driven approaches, product managers can effectively measure product success, make informed decisions, and drive continuous improvement. Understanding and applying these principles helps ensure that product initiatives align with strategic goals, meet user needs, and deliver valuable outcomes. Embracing a data-driven mindset and utilizing relevant metrics empowers product managers to navigate the complexities of their role and achieve long-term success in a competitive market.

CHAPTER ELEVEN

CAREER DEVELOPMENT AND GROWTH AS A PRODUCT MANAGER

Navigating the journey of a product management career involves understanding the various pathways for advancement and the importance of continuous skills development. This fascinating field offers numerous opportunities for growth, ranging from expanding responsibilities to moving into specialized or senior roles. To thrive in this profession, individuals must continuously refine their skills and seek out new learning opportunities.

Pathways for Advancement

Embarking on a career in product management often begins with entry-level positions, such as Associate Product Manager. In this role, professionals support senior team members and work on specific projects or features. This foundational position is crucial for building a strong understanding of the field and preparing for increased responsibilities. As one gains experience and demonstrates their abilities, the next step typically involves advancing to a Product Manager role. This position requires taking on more substantial responsibilities, such as leading product development efforts and managing cross-functional teams. A successful transition to this role involves not only managing projects but also driving strategic decisions and aligning with broader organizational goals.

For those looking to further advance, the Senior Product Manager role represents a significant step forward. In this capacity, individuals oversee a larger scope of products or features, develop strategic plans, and often mentor junior team members. Senior professionals are expected to have a deeper grasp of market dynamics and user needs, playing a key role in shaping the product vision and ensuring its alignment with company objectives.

The journey may continue with a move into a Group Product Manager position, which involves managing a portfolio of products or leading a larger team of product managers. This role demands a strategic oversight of multiple products, resource allocation, and ensuring that the product portfolio aligns with organizational strategies. Group Product Managers are tasked with setting broader strategies and driving overall product success.

Reaching the Director of Product Management level involves taking on a senior leadership role, overseeing the entire product management function within the organization. Directors are responsible for defining the strategic direction for the product portfolio, managing a team, and collaborating with other executives to drive company-wide initiatives. This role requires a blend of strategic thinking and leadership skills.

The journey can culminate in roles such as Vice President of Product Management or Chief Product Officer (CPO). VPs oversee high-level strategy and organizational leadership, setting the overall vision for the product portfolio and working closely with other C-level executives. The CPO role represents the pinnacle of the career ladder, responsible for the overall product strategy and vision, leading the product management organization, and driving innovation across the company. For those interested in specialization, roles such as Product Design Lead, UX Director, or Head of Product Analytics offer opportunities to focus on specific areas. Specialization allows for developing deep expertise in particular domains, which can be valuable for consulting roles or thought leadership positions. Additionally, entrepreneurship offers a unique path for applying product management skills to create new ventures, while adjacent roles in business development or strategy provide alternative avenues for leveraging product management expertise.

Skills Development and Continuing Education

To succeed and advance in this field, ongoing skills development and education are essential. As the field evolves, staying current with new tools, methodologies, and best practices is crucial. Mastery of core skills, including product lifecycle management, market research, user experience design, and project management, forms the foundation of a successful career. Refining these skills through practical experience and formal training ensures continued effectiveness in managing and developing products.

Embracing new tools and technologies is also vital. The field is increasingly driven by advanced tools for data analytics, product development, and project management. Staying proficient with these tools enhances efficiency and effectiveness. Pursuing advanced education, such as an MBA or specialized courses in relevant areas, can provide valuable knowledge and credentials, opening doors to higher-level roles and offering a competitive edge.

Attending industry conferences and workshops provides opportunities to learn from experts, network with peers, and stay informed about the latest trends. Participating in these events helps individuals gain insights into emerging practices and engage with thought leaders. Certifications related to product management, offered by institutions, can validate skills and knowledge, enhancing credibility and career prospects. Mentorship and coaching from experienced professionals offer valuable guidance and support. Engaging with a mentor or coach can accelerate personal growth, provide feedback, and help navigate career challenges. Peer learning groups and communities facilitate knowledge sharing and collaboration, offering fresh perspectives and practical solutions to common challenges.

Developing soft skills, such as leadership, communication, and negotiation, is equally important. Strong leadership skills are essential for managing teams and influencing stakeholders, while effective communication and negotiation are crucial for advocating product needs and building relationships. Self-directed learning, through exploring new topics, reading relevant books, or completing online courses, helps stay current with industry developments and continuously improve skills.

Regular reflection on personal experiences and applying learnings to current projects is a key aspect of ongoing development. Assessing what worked well, identifying areas for improvement, and applying insights to future endeavors reinforces skills and adapts to new challenges effectively.

Building a Personal Brand and Professional Network

In this competitive field, building a personal brand and cultivating a strong professional network are crucial for career advancement. Establishing a personal brand involves showcasing your unique strengths, expertise, and achievements in a way that distinguishes you from others. This can be achieved through various means, including creating a compelling online presence, contributing to industry blogs or publications, and speaking at conferences or webinars. A well-defined personal brand not only enhances your visibility but also positions you as a thought leader in the field.

Building a robust professional network is equally important. Networking with peers, mentors, and industry leaders provides opportunities for career growth, knowledge exchange, and potential collaborations. Attending industry events, joining professional organizations, and engaging in online communities are effective ways to expand your network. By actively participating in these networks, you can gain valuable insights, stay informed about industry trends, and discover new career opportunities. A strong network can also provide support and advice, helping you navigate career challenges and make informed decisions.

Navigating Organizational Politics and Building Influence

Understanding and effectively navigating organizational politics is a key skill for advancing in product management. Organizational politics refers to the dynamics and power structures within a company that can impact decision-making and career progression. Building influence involves developing relationships with key stakeholders, understanding their motivations, and aligning your efforts with the company's strategic goals. This requires a combination of strategic communication, negotiation skills, and the ability to advocate for your initiatives effectively.

Developing influence within a company involves demonstrating value through successful project outcomes, building alliances with influential colleagues, and effectively communicating the impact of your work. By navigating organizational politics skillfully, you can gain support for your ideas, advance your career, and contribute more effectively to the company's success.

Building influence within an institution requires a strategic approach to relationship management and communication. Start by understanding the motivations and priorities of key stakeholders and aligning your initiatives with their interests. Effective communication is crucial; clearly articulate how your projects contribute to the organization's goals and demonstrate their value through tangible outcomes. Building alliances with influential colleagues can also bolster your position and facilitate support for your initiatives. Cultivating trust and credibility through consistent performance and collaboration will help you gain the backing needed to advance your career and drive organizational success.

Handling organizational challenges involves navigating complex power dynamics and addressing conflicts constructively. Stay aware of the internal politics and power structures that can impact decision-making and project outcomes. Develop a proactive approach to problem-solving by engaging with stakeholders early, managing expectations, and negotiating effectively. By maintaining a focus on the broader organizational goals and demonstrating your ability to overcome obstacles, you can build a reputation as a resilient and influential leader. This wise handling of challenges not only enhances your career prospects but also strengthens your role within the organization.

Growth in the field of product management involves navigating various career paths and continuously developing skills. From starting in entry-level positions to advancing to senior roles, the journey requires a combination of experience, strategic thinking, and ongoing education. By embracing continuous learning, staying current with industry trends, and developing both technical and soft skills, professionals can build a rewarding and impactful career. This approach ensures that individuals remain relevant, effective, and poised for long-term success in this ever-evolving sector.

CHAPTER TWELEVE

FUTURE TRENDS IN PRODUCT MANAGEMENT

As product management continues to evolve, staying ahead of emerging trends and technologies is crucial for maintaining a competitive edge and driving innovation. This chapter explores the latest trends shaping the role of product managers and offers strategies for staying ahead in a rapidly changing field.

Emerging Trends and Technologies Shaping the Role

Artificial Intelligence and Machine Learning

Artificial intelligence (AI) and machine learning (ML) are transforming how products are developed, optimized, and delivered. AI-driven tools are increasingly being used for data analysis, predictive analytics, and personalization. Product managers are leveraging these technologies to gain deeper insights into user behavior, forecast market trends, and tailor products to individual needs. Machine learning algorithms enable products to learn from user interactions and improve over time, enhancing the overall user experience.

The integration of AI and ML into product development processes can also streamline workflows, automate repetitive tasks, and optimize resource allocation. For instance, AI-powered chatbots can handle customer service inquiries, allowing teams to focus on more complex issues. As these technologies advance, product managers need to stay informed about their capabilities and limitations, ensuring they can effectively integrate them into their product strategies.

Data-Driven Decision Making

The reliance on data to guide product decisions is becoming more pronounced. Advanced analytics platforms and big data technologies enable product managers to gather and analyze vast amounts of data from various sources. This data-driven approach helps in identifying user needs, tracking product performance, and making informed decisions about feature development and prioritization.

Real-time analytics tools are increasingly important, allowing product managers to make quick adjustments based on current user behavior and market conditions. By harnessing data effectively, product managers can improve product design, enhance user experiences, and drive business outcomes. The challenge lies in not only collecting and analyzing data but also translating insights into actionable strategies.

Remote and Distributed Teams

The rise of remote and distributed workforces is reshaping how product teams operate. Advances in communication and collaboration tools have made it possible for teams to work effectively from different locations around the world. Product managers must navigate the complexities of managing remote teams, ensuring that communication remains clear, and collaboration is seamless.

Tools like Slack, Microsoft Teams, and Asana facilitate real-time communication and project management, while video conferencing platforms like Zoom and Google Meet enable face-to-face interactions. Product managers need to be adept at using these tools to maintain team cohesion, manage projects efficiently, and drive productivity despite geographical distances.

Agile and Lean Methodologies

Agile and lean methodologies continue to evolve and influence product management practices. Agile principles, such as iterative development and continuous feedback, enable teams to respond quickly to changes and deliver incremental value. Lean methodologies focus on minimizing waste and maximizing value by validating assumptions and prioritizing customer needs.

Product managers are increasingly adopting hybrid approaches that combine elements of both methodologies to tailor processes to their specific needs. Embracing these approaches requires a mindset shift towards flexibility, experimentation, and rapid iteration, ensuring that products remain relevant and aligned with user needs.

User-Centric Design and Experience

The emphasis on user-centric design and experience is stronger than ever. Product managers are prioritizing user research and design thinking to create products that meet user needs and deliver exceptional experiences. This trend involves deep understanding of user pain points, preferences, and behaviors, and incorporating these insights into product design and development.

Tools for user testing, feedback collection, and usability analysis are becoming more sophisticated, enabling product managers to gather valuable input throughout the product lifecycle. By focusing on user experience (UX) and incorporating user feedback, product managers can create products that resonate with their target audience and drive higher satisfaction and engagement.

Ethical and Inclusive Design

There is a growing emphasis on ethical and inclusive design in product development. Product managers are increasingly aware of the need to consider the broader societal impact of their products and ensure they are accessible and inclusive to diverse user groups. This trend involves addressing issues such as data privacy, algorithmic bias, and accessibility.

Ethical design practices require product managers to consider the potential consequences of their decisions and ensure that products are designed with fairness, transparency, and inclusiveness in mind. This includes implementing features that accommodate users with disabilities, protecting user data, and avoiding biases in AI and machine learning algorithms.

Integration of Internet of Things (IoT)

The integration of Internet of Things (IoT) technologies is expanding the scope of product management. IoT devices are becoming increasingly prevalent in various sectors, from smart homes to industrial applications. Product managers need to understand how to manage interconnected products and ensure they work seamlessly within an ecosystem of devices.

Managing IoT products involves addressing challenges related to data security, interoperability, and user privacy. Product experts must also consider how to integrate IoT data into product development processes and leverage it to enhance functionality and user experience.

Sustainability and Green Product Development

Sustainability is becoming a significant factor in full cycle development and management. Consumers are increasingly demanding environmentally friendly products and companies are responding by focusing on sustainable practices. This includes using eco-friendly materials, reducing carbon footprints, and implementing circular economy principles.

Product managers are tasked with balancing sustainability goals with product performance and cost considerations. This trend involves incorporating sustainable practices into the product lifecycle, from design and manufacturing to distribution and disposal.

Blockchain Technology

Blockchain technology is making waves beyond its initial use in crypto currencies. Its applications in product management include enhancing transparency, security, and traceability. It can be used for secure transactions, supply chain management, and verifying product authenticity.

Product experts and teams need to understand how this technology can be applied to their products and evaluate its potential benefits and limitations. This requires staying informed about developments in the area and exploring how it can be integrated into product strategies.

Personalization and Customization

Personalization and customization are key trends in delivering tailored experiences to users. Advances in data analytics and machine learning enable product managers to create highly personalized products and services that cater to individual preferences and behaviors.

By leveraging data to provide personalized recommendations, content, and experiences, product managers can enhance user satisfaction and engagement. Customization options allow users to tailor products to their specific needs, further increasing their value and appeal.

How to Stay Ahead in a Rapidly Evolving Field

Staying ahead in the fast-paced field of product management requires **a proactive approach to learning and adaptation.** Here are some strategies to ensure you remain at the forefront of industry developments:

Continuous Learning and Professional Development: Engaging in continuous learning is essential for keeping up with emerging trends and technologies. This involves attending industry conferences, participating in webinars, and enrolling in relevant courses or certifications. Staying updated with the latest research, tools, and methodologies helps you adapt to changes and apply new knowledge to your role.

Networking and Industry Engagement: Building a strong professional network can provide valuable insights and opportunities. Engage with industry peers, join professional organizations, and participate in online forums or communities. Networking with experts and thought leaders can offer fresh perspectives, keep you informed about industry trends, and open doors to new career opportunities.

Embracing Change and Innovation: Adopting a mindset that embraces change and innovation is crucial for staying ahead. Be open to experimenting with new tools, methodologies, and technologies. Foster a culture of experimentation within your team and encourage innovative thinking. By proactively seeking out and embracing new approaches, you can drive progress and stay ahead of competitors.

Developing Cross-Functional Skills: Cultivating cross-functional skills can enhance your ability to manage diverse aspects of product development. Skills such as data analysis, design thinking, and agile methodologies are increasingly valuable. Expanding your expertise beyond traditional product management can help you adapt to various challenges and contribute more effectively to your organization.

Seeking Mentorship and Guidance: Engaging with mentors or industry experts can provide personalized guidance and support. Mentorship offers opportunities to gain insights from experienced professionals, receive feedback on your career development, and navigate complex challenges. Seeking guidance from those with a wealth of experience can accelerate your growth and help you make informed decisions.

Staying Informed of Industry Trends: Regularly consume industry publications, blogs, and news sources to stay informed about the latest developments. Subscribe to newsletters, follow thought leaders on social media, and participate in relevant online discussions. Staying informed helps you anticipate changes, understand emerging trends, and adapt your strategies accordingly.

Implementing Agile Learning Strategies: Adopt agile learning strategies to continuously improve and adapt. Implement iterative learning approaches where you regularly assess your skills, gather feedback, and make incremental improvements. This approach helps you stay adaptable and responsive to changes in the field.

Fostering a Culture of Continuous Improvement: Promote a culture of continuous improvement within your team or organization. Encourage feedback, regularly review processes, and seek opportunities for enhancement. By fostering a culture that values learning and development, you can drive innovation and maintain a competitive edge.

Leveraging Technology and Tools: Take advantage of technology and tools that can enhance your productivity and effectiveness. Explore new software, platforms, and systems that can streamline your workflows, facilitate collaboration, and provide valuable insights. Staying proficient with the latest tools ensures you can leverage their capabilities to drive success.

Balancing Long-Term Vision with Short-Term Goals: While staying informed about emerging trends, balance your focus on long-term vision with short-term goals. Develop strategies that align with both immediate needs and future aspirations. This balanced approach ensures you remain agile and responsive while working towards overarching objectives.

As the field of product management continues to evolve, staying ahead of emerging trends and technologies is crucial for maintaining a competitive edge. By embracing advancements such as AI, data-driven decision-making, and agile methodologies, and by adopting strategies for continuous learning and adaptation, you can navigate the dynamic landscape effectively. Cultivating a proactive approach to professional development, networking, and innovation will position you for success in a rapidly changing field, ensuring that you remain at the forefront of product management and drive meaningful impact within your organization.

CHAPTER THIRTEEN
FINAL THOUGHTS

Embarking on a career as a product manager is both an exhilarating and challenging journey. Throughout this book, we've explored the multifaceted role of a product manager and the compelling reasons why this career path can be deeply fulfilling. From understanding the core responsibilities and skills required to navigating career development and staying ahead in a rapidly evolving field, we've touched on key aspects that define the essence of product management.

We began by delving into the fundamental aspects of product management, highlighting how a product manager's role is central to guiding products from conception through to market success. The ability to manage cross-functional teams, prioritize tasks, and make strategic decisions is vital. This role demands a unique blend of analytical thinking, creativity, and interpersonal skills. It's about balancing user needs with business goals and continuously iterating to improve the product. We discussed the importance of creating and communicating a clear product vision and strategy, emphasizing the need to align product goals with broader business objectives. Crafting a compelling vision that resonates with both your team and stakeholders is crucial for driving a product's success.

As we progressed, we examined the practical aspects of managing product roadmaps and prioritization. We explored techniques for effective roadmap creation, balancing short-term needs with long-term goals, and incorporating stakeholder input. The essence of successful product management lies in making informed decisions that not only address immediate concerns but also pave the way for future growth. It's about prioritizing features and improvements that align with your product's strategic vision while remaining adaptable to changing market conditions.

We also tackled the complexities of navigating challenges and making tough decisions. The journey of a product manager is rarely smooth; it is filled with obstacles and difficult choices. From handling conflicting priorities to managing stakeholder expectations, the strategies for overcoming these challenges are integral to thriving in this role. Utilizing decision-making frameworks and tools can provide structure and clarity, helping to guide you through the uncertainty and pressure that often accompany product management.

The chapter on career development and growth offered insights into the pathways available within the field. Whether starting in an entry-level position or aiming for a senior leadership role, the opportunities for advancement are diverse. We discussed the importance of continuous skills development, staying updated with industry trends, and building a strong professional network. Career progression in product management involves not only honing technical and strategic skills but also developing leadership and communication abilities that can set you apart.

Our exploration of future trends highlighted the importance of staying ahead in a rapidly changing landscape. With emerging technologies like artificial intelligence, machine learning, and big data shaping the future of product management, it's essential to be proactive in learning and adapting. Embracing new methodologies, fostering a culture of innovation, and leveraging technology are key to staying relevant and driving impactful results.

In conclusion, the journey of becoming a product manager is a blend of excitement, challenge, and continuous growth. It's a role that offers the opportunity to shape products that have the potential to make a significant impact on users' lives and the market. By understanding the core responsibilities, developing essential skills, and staying attuned to industry trends, you can embark on a rewarding career that not only aligns with your professional aspirations but also fuels your passion for creating and innovating.

So, why should you be a product manager? Because it's a role that allows you to be at the forefront of innovation, driving products from concept to reality. It offers the chance to lead diverse teams, solve complex problems, and make a tangible difference in the world. If you're passionate about shaping the future and thrive in a dynamic environment, product management could be the perfect path for you. Embrace the challenges, seize the opportunities, and step confidently into a career where your impact can be profound and lasting.

www.ingramcontent.com/pod-product-compliance
Lightning Source LLC
LaVergne TN
LVHW061527070526
838199LV00009B/407